New Lawyer Launch

New Lawyer Launch

The Handbook for Young Lawyers

Susan Smith Blakely, Esquire

fastcase FULL COURT PRESS

 For customer support, please contact Fastcase, Inc., 711 D St. NW, Suite 200, Washington, DC 20004, 202.999.4777 (phone), 202.521.3462 (fax), or email customer service at support@fastcase.com.

A Full Court Press, Fastcase, Inc., Publication.

Printed and bound in the United States of America.

10 9 8 7 6 5 4 3 2 1

ISBN (print): 978-1-949884-84-5
ISBN (online): 978-1-949884-85-2

This book's cover image is credited to CSA-Archive: https://www.istockphoto.com/vector/rocket-gm530615361-54943778?irgwc=1&cid=IS&utm_medium=affiliate&utm_source=freevector.com&clickid=TwoSjIwQOxyNR-RxPKQnk1kzUkDQwwylIx4x3U0&utm_term=freevector.com&utm_campaign=SRP&utm_content=1141943&irpid=39452

The title page image is by Freepik: https://www.freepik.com/free-vector/gradient-galaxy-background_14658088.htm#query=galaxy&position=15&from_view=keyword

This book is dedicated to all young lawyers who value their professions and appreciate mentoring. They are the future leaders of a profession in transition.

Contents

Foreword

Susan Blakely's books in the Best Friends at the Bar series are must reads for young lawyers. Her wisdom, knowledge, experience, and insight serve as useful guides to those entering the law profession, and this fifth book is no exception. *New Lawyer Launch: The Handbook for Young Lawyers* is an easily digestible handbook that makes it clear that Susan Blakely knows of what she speaks.

This is no surprise to me. I have known Susan for decades, and I know that this work is not just a job or a task for Susan. It is a true commitment, a mission. More than anything, she wants young lawyers to do well and have success in a profession she loves.

Why are her books so valuable and useful? Susan shares not only her own extensive experience as lawyer in private practice, teacher, lecturer, and manager in the public sector but also the experience and wisdom of other lawyers of varying ages from a wide variety of practice experiences. She focuses on the private practice of law, but all of her insights are relevant to the wider spectrum of jobs in which young lawyers may engage. And, while many of the book topics and her recommendations may seem self-evident, like the Declaration of Independence, they merit repeating and highlighting and are ever new and applicable.

Very appropriately she starts the book by asking the reader whether he or she became a lawyer for the right reasons and what to do if the answer is in the negative. That triggers my recollection of hearing Dean William Treanor of Susan's and my law school, Georgetown, ask students to reflect on whether they went to law school primarily to earn a substantial income. Dean Treanor argues, and I think effectively, that is not a sufficient reason. The practice of law may provide a very comfortable living, but, if a lawyer really wants to get rich, he or she should actively consider venture-capital or joining a hedge fund. Being men and women for others is a much more satisfying use of a law degree. It is not necessary to be counsel to a not-for-profit to experience this, although that can be very personally rewarding. For example, I have spent most of my professional life in Big Law. I believe practice in a large multinational law firm can lead to personal satisfaction and a justified feeling that clients have benefited from effective, prudent, ethical, and thoughtful counsel from the lawyers in that setting.

Highlighting one or two of Susan's topics risks neglecting the many other important suggestions she makes. However, I will mention just two: (1) be respectful to the staff and (2) show initiative and act like an owner.

I recall a Georgetown Law alumni luncheon many years ago when our mutual Georgetown Law graduate Greta Van Susteren told the audience how she got her break as a television commentator. It was because she had been kind and considerate to a secretary! That's how her significant career as a television legal commentator was born.

And while it is obviously important to do all assignments well, acting like an owner can reap large benefits. The partner giving the young lawyer an assignment may not have thought through all of the issues and implications and could very well appreciate suggestions of how a memo or a brief might perhaps have a different focus or highlight a different issue. Looking at it from the perspective of the partner, and ultimately the client, should produce a better work product.

And there is so much more. It is my pleasure to introduce you to the nuggets and pearls of wisdom Susan Blakely has provided the readers of this book. The lessons learned here will reverberate for years to come.

Marcia A. Wiss
Managing Partner of Wiss & Partners LLP
Retired partner from Hogan Lovells

Acknowledgments

As I have done for every book in the Best Friends at the Bar series, I thank my family of lawyers, including my husband and our two children, for their patience and understanding of my mission and my passion on behalf of young lawyers. The role that my family members play as sounding boards for my work is invaluable to me and the success of the Best Friends at the Bar project.

I also thank my "almost family" who urged me to write this book and have served as advisors and counselors to me at every turn during the evolution of Best Friends at the Bar. They know who they are and that their encouragement and support have been central to the success of my programs.

I also am very grateful for the contributors to this book, who have faith in the project and took the time to provide input to assure the best possible and up-to-date advice for young lawyers. I understand how important it is for young lawyers to know that Generation X and Millennial Generation lawyers, who walked in their shoes not so long ago, are among those speaking to them through this book.

The book contributors are:

- Libby Baney, Partner, Faegre Drinker Biddle & Reath LLP

- William D. Blakely, Principal, William Blakely Law PLLC, and formerly Partner, Polsinelli and DLA Piper LLP
- Thomas M. Brownell, Partner, Holland & Knight
- Victoria Bruno, Partner, Womble Bond Dickinson (US) LLP
- Marjorie Burchett, Principal, Marjorie Burchett Law, and formerly Dentons and Luce Forward
- Antonio Calabrese, Partner, DLA Piper LLP (US)
- Scott L. Fredericksen, Partner, Foley & Lardner LLP
- George E. Kostel, Managing Principal, Impresa Legal Group and formerly Partner, Polsinelli, Nelson Mullins and Reed Smith
- Jordan E. Langlois, Partner, Kornfeld LLP
- Monica McCabe, formerly Chair of the Intellectual Property Department at Phillips Nizer LLP
- Anthony Nasharr, Partner, Polsinelli
- Christopher Schafbuch, Associate, Lowenstein Sandler LLP
- Crystal Y'Barbo Stapely, formerly Of Counsel, Vinson & Elkins LLP
- Brian Tennebaum, Special Counsel, Bast Amron LLP
- Brian Winterhalter, Of Counsel, DLA Piper LLP (US)

Introduction

Welcome to the *New Lawyer Launch.* You will find everything you need to know here as you begin or continue your career in the practice of law.

This book focuses on the practical and strategic things that you likely did not learn in law school or in your internships, externships, or even your summer associate experiences but are critical to your success in law firm practice. They are the very things that can trip up young lawyers and get them off to very shaky starts. Having this information will prepare you for the obstacles and pitfalls that lie ahead—but can be avoided.

You will learn what it means to be a lawyer and to "practice law" far beyond the diploma and bar swearing-in ceremony, and you will get invaluable strategies for survival and success from contributors to this book who "walk the walk" and "talk the talk" on a daily basis. They are the Generation X and Millennial lawyers, who understand what it takes to get ahead in the profession and have joined me to provide "up-to-date" advice from their experiences in law firms of all sizes, including solo and virtual practices. They are listed in the Acknowledgments, and I am sure you will agree that they are an impressive group. You are fortunate to have them helping you out with the generosity of their time and talent.

I understand that each one of you is different and that you all will have individual approaches to the way you practice law. I understand this because of the many lawyers I have known and worked with during my career—each who had unique approaches to the profession. However, the one thing that all those lawyers, who have played major roles in my career, have in common is that they all wish that, *once upon a time*, they had been given a book like this one.

And that is why I wrote this book for you. Because I do not believe in hiding the ball and making a "survival of the fittest" game of practicing law. I think it is a waste of your time and certainly a waste of clients' money. I prefer a candid and transparent approach that recognizes the complexity of the profession and your eagerness to learn and prosper.

This book is a logical extension of the work I have done on behalf of young lawyers for well over a decade. The Best Friends at the Bar books include *What Women Need to Know About a Career in the Law* (2009), *The New Balance for Today's Woman Lawyer* (2012), and *Top-Down Leadership for Women Lawyers* (2015). Those books address the retention and advancement of women lawyers, the challenges that women lawyers face in what continues to be a male-dominated profession, and the responsibility for leadership to help women lawyers meet and overcome those challenges.

More recently, I turned my attentions to millennial lawyers and the unique challenges they face in a profession that does not necessarily mirror their values. *What Millennial Lawyers Want: A Bridge from the Past to the Future of Law Practice* (2018) was my first response to what I saw as serious discontent among so many young practitioners—not just women lawyers but young male practitioners as well. It started me on a new path, and this book is an extension of that work.

However, this book is different than the others. It is not gender or generation specific, and it is a handbook for easy reference and ready access to discreet information that will prove to be very important to you. The Contents is thorough and will allow you to get answers fast throughout your career when you confront a problem or see a promotional opportunity in front of you and need to scramble to meet the moment. Access to this information early in your career allows you to be prepared for what lies ahead.

The things that you will learn here are what senior lawyers believe are critical for you to know if you are serious about a law career. It is the information that will make your experience as a young lawyer so much less stressful and more enjoyable because you will understand what to expect and what is expected of you.

Here it is, at your fingertips. And your part of the bargain is simply to be honest about your strengths and weaknesses, and keep your mind open to all possibilities.

And if, after you take advantage of the lessons here and get some valuable experience under your belt, you find that your chosen career in the law or your chosen practice is *not* what you need, there is a chapter on transitions to help you create the career you want and one which will bring you satisfaction and fulfillment.

Throughout my practice years, the need for more effective mentoring of young lawyers became clear to me. So, when I retired from private practice in 2006, I founded the award-winning Best Friends at the Bar project to help young lawyers get started in the profession in a meaningful way. And this, my fifth book, continues that work.

In my role as a lecturer and consultant, I have mentored thousands of young lawyers as part of almost 100 presentations at law firms, law schools, and law organizations. I also have published articles in and been featured in a variety of legal media, including *ABA Journal* (as a monthly columnist), *National Jurist*, *Corporate Counsel* magazine, the *LA Daily Journal*, *Forbes Woman*, *Lawyerist.com*, *Daily Muse*, *Lawyer and Statesman*, *Huffington Post Business*, and *Law360.* My website also includes hundreds of blogs and access to Best Friends at the Bar newsletters on issues related to developing successful law careers.

I have been known to reach well beyond the law for inspiration, and this is one of those times. The famous architect I.M. Pei, who designed the John F. Kennedy Library and the Hancock Tower in Boston as well as many other notable buildings around the world, is quoted as saying that "Success is a collection of problems solved." He believed that challenges helped to toughen him as an architect, and his example stands to remind me always that satisfaction at the finish line has its foundation in the challenges that are overcome along the way.

So, let's get started on the *New Lawyer Launch* where we will address the law profession challenges that lie ahead for you and prepare to overcome them.

About the Author

Susan Smith Blakely is a teacher, lawyer, and award-winning author for the Best Friends at the Bar project. During her more than 25 practice years, including as an associate, of counsel, and partner, Ms. Blakely specialized in infrastructure construction litigation and land use and development law. She also served in the public sector as a chief of staff for an elected official. Ms. Blakely holds a Bachelor's degree from the University of Wisconsin and a Juris Doctorate from Georgetown Law, where she also was a teaching fellow for 1Ls.

This is Ms. Blakely's fifth book in the Best Friends at the Bar series. Her prior book titles are *What Women Need to Know About a Career in the Law* (2009), *The New Balance for Today's Woman Lawyer* (2012), *Top-Down Leadership for Women Lawyers* (2015), and *What Millennial Lawyers Want* (2018). She speaks at law schools, law firms, and law organizations and counsels individual lawyers. Recently she presented her ninety-seventh program to a defense lawyers association.

Ms. Blakely lives in Northern Virginia outside of Washington, DC, with her husband, who also is a lawyer. They have two children, one a partner in an Am Law 100 firm and the other an Assistant United States Attorney.

New Lawyer Launch

Chapter One

You're a Lawyer Now—What Does That Mean?

You lived through law school, graduated, went to commencement and celebrated your successes (I hope!), and passed the bar exam. You either have been practicing for a few years or you are about to begin your legal career.

Congratulations! These are great accomplishments. You have joined a distinguished profession and one that I hope fits you well. But you still have many questions.

Some of the questions I hear repeatedly from young lawyers are "What does *being* a lawyer really mean? What are the realities of law practice today? What kind of behavior is expected of a lawyer? How do you learn the ropes and become successful? What are the pitfalls to success?"

They are all good questions and need to be answered. But, typically, your experiences in law school did not prepare you to answer them. Law school did not focus on the realities of law practice and the critical question "What kind of behavior and commitment to profession must a lawyer demonstrate to become successful and have a satisfying career?"

Law school taught you the elements of torts and crimes and the fundamentals of contracts, property law, estates and trusts, and other substantive and procedural areas of the law, and you also learned about ethical behavior. But there was not a course on becoming successful or finding satisfaction in the practice of law. "Work hard and master core competency skills" is probably as close as you got to an answer about the realities of law practice. And, clearly, that is not enough.

To adequately answer questions related to the realities of law practice and becoming successful in the profession, we need to start by talking candidly about law practice. And not just as an academic exercise. Success and failure are very real outcomes and require a more serious approach.

Generally speaking, the practice of law is very hard and demanding work. It requires fine tuning the substantive and procedural law that you learned in law school, mastering both oral and written communications, negotiating successfully on behalf of yourself and clients, and navigating relationships with staff, colleagues, supervisors, clients, opposing counsel, and judges. There is a lot to learn, and the pace can be hectic. There is little time for foolishness and fundamental errors in judgment.

Here are some of the truths and harsh realities about law practice. It can interfere with your personal life, and it can make you feel like a slave to your job. Most young lawyers did not anticipate how they would feel when they were in the office all weekend pouring over documents and missing fun with friends and family. They did not anticipate how they would feel when they missed a child's birthday party and a much-needed family vacation. They did not anticipate how it would feel to be caught in trial for weeks and months halfway across the country while the world went on without them. They did not understand the fine tap dance that goes on with difficult colleagues and managers to get the job done. And they did not understand the close relationship between unhappiness in professional lives and unhappiness in personal lives.

But those unvarnished truths represent only one side of the coin. There is another side of law practice, the side that can be exciting, gratifying, rewarding, and satisfying.

That other side is founded in the importance of the work that lawyers do, the benefits they can confer, the people they serve to make hopes and dreams come true, the lives they save from a harsh world and an unfair legal system, the wrongs they can right, and the myriad ways they can help to create an environmentally healthier and more beautiful world—to name just a few of the right reasons to become a lawyer. Those things may sound too aspirational to you, but they are truly what will turn a demanding pursuit in the law into a satisfying one.

Although it is true that you are likely to find untenable workload requirements, long hours, leaders who are out of touch with current societal mores and behaviors, and law practice cultures that fall short of your expectations, you also are likely to find important work that needs to be done and professional satisfaction beyond your wildest dreams. There are so many possibilities for those who learn the ropes and craft careers with purpose.

So, how do you avoid the pitfalls, justify the hardships, and get to the satisfying part? That is a critical question, and you will find information in this book that gets to the heart of the answer.

As you read, you will discover that most fundamental errors in law practice center on unfortunate behaviors and the lack of wisdom behind those behaviors. You will discover that there are critical behaviors and strategies that you must master and demonstrate every step of your career. There also are certain behaviors that are unacceptable, and you must learn to identify them and overcome them if you want to succeed.

There is no question that you are smart and capable, but the objective here is to make you wise and to help you make good decisions to avoid tripping over yourself on the way to your success. The goal is to get you started toward the finish line in a wiser, smoother, more professional way and to spare you embarrassment and humiliation. If you dedicate yourself to achieving that goal, you will be a much happier and satisfied lawyer.

That kind of preparation starts with you thinking critically about your workplace and how you fit in there. You need to understand the structure of the organization, the way business is done, and what the expectations are for you within that organization.

Many of you may be Millennial Generation lawyers, born generally between 1980 and 2000. Research shows that millennial lawyers, stereotypically, have experiences and characteristics which can become serious impediments to achieving success in law practice. For example, many millennials were raised by helicopter parents, who praised them to the extreme and did not prepare them well for the kind of constructive criticism they encounter as entry-level lawyers.

Millennials also were raised with an abundance of Internet exposure compared with prior generations. They became accustomed to communicating on platforms like Facebook and Twitter and gained only limited experience or confidence with face-to-face communication and relationship building.

Millennials also lived through the tragedy of 9/11 and two economic recessions. They saw parents lose jobs and families lose homes. Those experiences created insecurities and aversion to risk that can be limiting professionally.

The research about millennials is included in much greater detail in my book *What Millennial Lawyers Want* in a format that includes millennial lawyers talking about the problems they have faced in pursuing law careers. I found the descriptions of their challenges in their own words to be compelling, but I also found many of their expectations to be unreasonable as they relate to law practice today.

The life experiences described above have left many millennials at a loss where law practice is concerned. Some of these young lawyers also have had only limited access to practitioner role models and effective mentors, and they have been disadvantaged in developing effective methods of communication and conflict resolution without those experiences. As a result, Millennial Generation lawyers, and perhaps Generation Z lawyers, who share some of the same characteristics, are having trouble fitting into the traditional practice of law.

The result is frustration by both the young lawyers and practice leaders and managers. Everybody complains. The young lawyers think they are being ignored, treated unfairly, and judged harshly, and the seasoned lawyers scratch their heads trying to respond to values and issues they do not understand.

And the frustrations experienced by young lawyers are causing them to leave the profession in record numbers. As reported in Thompson Reuter's "2022 State of the Legal Market,"[1] the "great resignation" saw a record high 23.2% associate turnover in 2021. It is speculated in the report that the result was not primarily driven by compensation issues but, rather, the main concern was lack of flexibility and personal control over working arrangements.

Another 2021 survey reported in *The American Lawyer* found that 60% of the associates surveyed would consider

[1] https://iltanet.org/blogs/maureen-blando/2022/02/03/dont-miss-thomson-reuters-2022-report-on-the-state.

leaving their firms for an improved work-life balance—and now 25% of associates have done just that in recent months.[2]

Others look at the current turnover differently and call it "The Great Reflection." This perspective is best described in a *Law.com Barometer* article from February 2022 as follows:

> The Shift: Is the "Great Resignation" Really the "Great Reflection"?
>
> So much is being discussed around the ongoing talent war and specifically the 'Great Resignation.' But as a recent contributor to Corporate Counsel pointed out—maybe it should really be called the 'Great Reflection' due to the fact that we're not seeing lawyers question whether they should be practicing law, but rather reflecting on how, why, and for whom they practice it.
>
> "People expect more of their employer today," said Betsy Tucci, general counsel of Los Angeles-based InStride. "It is not just the place where you show up and you do your 8-5, and you go home. It is a community, it is an enabler, it is an opportunity to make an impact."[3]

Yet another article in *Above the Law*, "Young Lawyers in Trouble" by James Goodnow,[4] addresses the results of a

---

[2] https://www.law.com/americanlawyer/2021/08/23/midlevel-associates-arent-satisfied-with-law-firms-return-to-office-plans/.

[3] Heather Nevitt, "Is the 'Great Resignation' Really the 'Great Reflection'?" (Feb. 10, 2022), https://www.law.com/2022/02/10/is-the-great-resignation-really-the-great-reflection/.

[4] https://abovethelaw.com/2022/02/young-lawyers-in-trouble/.

recent survey commissioned by the International Bar Association demonstrating an alarming and disturbing level of workplace dissatisfaction among young lawyers. One out of three survey respondents said they were likely to move on to a new branch of the legal profession, and 20% of respondents reported they were likely to leave the practice of law altogether. Most significant among those findings, for the purposes of this book, is that 90% of young attorneys surveyed reported encountering barriers that they were not prepared for like work-life balance issues, lack of mentorship, and promotion issues.

And the Internet and social media testimonials from young lawyers make it clear that the dissatisfaction is present in many practice settings—not just in Big Law. It is happening in law firms of all sizes, and it is happening to government lawyers, prosecutors, in-house corporate counsels, and even public defenders.

We can speculate that this great resignation or reflection is happening because law practice has undergone radical changes during the past 20 years. Layers upon layers of an information age moving at warp speed, an increasingly litigious society, and transactional practices driven by almost frenzied global commercial activity are forcing those changes. For lawyers just entering the profession, it is hard to be prepared for all that change.

The COVID-19 pandemic and the accompanying isolation and emphasis on introspection also has affected the attitudes of young lawyers about their chosen profession. My hope is that the great dissatisfaction and exodus of young lawyers will abate over the next few years as our country pulls out of harsh COVID conditions, and I wish for a less stressful time that will allow young lawyers to fulfill the expectations for their personal lives and put their professional lives in proper perspective.

Work is work. It is not play. It is hard to get your head around that when there is no play.

But a high attrition rate for young lawyers does not have to be the result. Retreat is not the only option when faced with challenges. Preparing for the challenges and the ultimate victory is another option and one that should be employed far in advance of the retreat. And that is what this book is all about.

All of you have a choice. If you choose to work in the law, you must learn to work *smart* in the law. You must learn to successfully navigate the pitfalls and embrace a balance that will promote a satisfying and enjoyable career as a lawyer. Personal definitions of success are key. As I hear so many young people today say, "*you* do *you*."

But there are other thorny issues *not* within your control. Although this book is a reliable source on how young lawyers need to behave and perform to secure their places in the profession, it does not ignore the unfortunate fact that the profession continues to be controlled through policies developed by Baby Boomers, which are proving to be archaic in a rapidly evolving world and changed human expectations about the conditions surrounding work lives. The good news is that it is now a profession in transition—a profession that is being forced to take a truthful account of its culture and how that culture affects its future. And you can become an important voice in that conversation if you play your cards right.

I hope you can see that a book like this is needed more than ever right now. To prepare you for the challenges discussed above, we must take a deep dive into the strategies young lawyers need to engage for survival and success. Familiarizing yourself with these strategies and mastering them will significantly increase your level of confidence and your chances for success.

Chapter Two

Developing Strategies for Survival and Success

You will encounter many obstacles on your journey to becoming a competent lawyer. Law practice is controlled by leaders who bring backgrounds and experiences different from your own to the table. They have been raised with different attitudes about what is pleasurable about work and their own roles in shaping their professional and personal lives. Many of them may be discontent in practice, but they have taken fatalistic attitudes toward their careers.

As difficult as you may find working for people with these attitudes, you have a great opportunity to learn from them and apply those skills to your practice. The skills will make you competitive in your work, and your experiences in gaining those skills will give you prospective for bringing about the changes that will make law practice more compatible with your values.

And you never should lose sight that your values are important. If you are a millennial lawyer, I have a pretty good idea what those values are. The value of time spent with friends and family and a balanced lifestyle are important to you. Respect and decency and honorable behavior are important to you. Cooperation among colleagues and as a valuable member of a team is important to you. These all are very defensible values, and they should not be mutually exclusive with the successful practice of law.

For those who think that the profession cannot tolerate these softer and more human values, I say they are wrong. Those lawyers need to be honest with themselves and ask whether six-figure salaries for entry-level lawyers and run-away partner profits are more important to the future of the profession than improved work-life balances, less toxic work environments, and satisfied workforces. They need to ask whether an emphasis on kindness, compassion, understanding, and personal relationships would harm the practice of law or improve it for future generations.

Those questions should be asked, and the lawyers, who hold fast to traditional methods of practice, need to ask them. Some *will* ask them. Some *will* push a new agenda. And some will be pushed in those directions by young lawyers like you.

However, you should not get ahead of yourself. At this early point in your career, you must learn the rules and play by the rules until you gain enough experience and expertise to change the rules. You can do this by mastering the survival strategies in this chapter. How you employ these strategies with your own special sauce is entirely up to *you*, but *you* must be an active participant in the process. Nobody else can learn this for you.

The specific survival strategies that follow include the fundamental and the aspirational, and some of them may seem annoyingly mundane. They address professional behaviors, not legal substance, but mastering appropriate behaviors and strategies will make the learning curve for the substance easier and smoother. Learning to fit into an organization, be liked there, and becoming an asset there are big foundational steps. As one of my contributors, a law practice manager, has written:

> "Most of these strategies may be familiar, but they are presented here in a most practical and effective manner. Despite changes in technology and flexible work schedules, these lessons have been around for a while. They are the 'do's and don'ts' that I have seen (or learned the hard way) from being a young lawyer and then mentoring them."

The strategies included here are essential in effectively pursuing the path forward toward a successful career. If you pay attention to the strategies, you will create your *value* as an asset to the practice of law and to your practice setting. You will have demonstrated that you are a lawyer who the firm or the organization does not want to lose.

Once you have created value, then you are in a position to make the firm or the organization work *for you*. You will be in a position where your stock is high and you are able to negotiate some of the workplace conditions and terms that are important to your life.

Maybe those conditions and terms are related to where you perform your work. Maybe those conditions and terms have to do with what teams you want to join and the work you want to do. Maybe those conditions and terms are related to parental leave and childcare. If you have created value you will be much more successful in your negotiations to achieve the things that are important to you.

Be aware that much of the information presented here is specific to law firm practice, even though some of you may not choose or have chosen that career path. That is intentional because current statistics show that almost 50% of today's law school graduates begin their careers in law firms.[1]

---

[1] https://abovethelaw.com/2022/04/the-jobs-are-plentiful-for-recent-law-school-graduates/.

The importance of getting off to a strong start cannot be overstated. Whether you are in a law firm practice or in a not-for-profit practice or an in-house practice, or a variety of other practices, the rules of the road are similar if not the same.

Using the information and the strategies presented here to your advantage will help you decide whether the profession *is* for you and what practice setting(s) might work best for you. Using the strategies also will help you advance a perception of competence and excellence that will get the attention of leaders and managers and open up practice opportunities for you.

Get Off to a Strong Start

Getting off to a strong start cannot be underestimated. Everything else flows from that.

Make a Positive First Impression

Making a positive first impression—with partners, senior associates, clients, and staff—is critical to success because those first impressions last. Remember that you have only one chance to make a positive first impression. If you blow it, it is blown for good.

So, be on time. Dress appropriately. Be attentive and responsive. Be polite and cooperative and use good manners. As one of my contributors wrote, "Set yourself apart from other lawyers—be nice to people! It's not that hard, folks!!"

Forget about how you scored on the LSAT and where you went to law school. Don't talk about your experiences on the law review. That is old news. You are now one among equals in your entering associate class. Everyone is on equal footing. It is a new day.

And please do not complain about the size of your office or the noise from the break room down the hall. No one likes a complainer.

Recognize that you do not "own" your assistant or paralegal. They have to respond to the needs of others also and, likely, you are the one with the least seniority among those they serve.

Get out of your office or cubicle from Day One and make your presence known. Isolation is a big problem these days for young people, but do not allow it to become *your* big problem. Meet and dialogue with as many workplace colleagues as possible, including leaders. They are the ones who will determine your future. The last thing you want is for your name to come up at a partnership meeting and for no one to know who you are.

This is not the time to be shy and retiring. Get involved in the practice, volunteer for committees, and go to *every* social event. Ask a colleague to lunch. You can finish billing hours later and avoid becoming known as the anti-social and uninteresting newcomer.

I understand that this kind of outreach is much easier said than done for some of you. If you trend toward being introverted, getting out of your office and mingling is not easy for you. You do not look forward to mixing it up with the braggarts and bullies in the group, and for good reason. They offend your values.

But if you let them keep you from something you need, they win. So, suck it up, be brave, and tolerate them—with the confidence of knowing that if you find them offensive, others do as well.

And avoid trouble. As one of my contributors points out, don't try to be the life of the party at work events. Another contributor reminds you to be careful how much alcohol you drink at work events, including office lunches, dinners, and parties. Drinking alcohol in excess can create big problems, and there are plenty of career-defining stories to back that up. Every lawyer knows at least one of those stories, and most lawyers love to tell them over and over and over again. Those episodes are very hard to escape.

Be appropriate in every way, and do not try too hard to be one of the cool people. Just be yourself—the best version of yourself.

Get Organized

And get organized asap! You may have heard that a messy office is the sign of a person with an active mind. That could be true, but it also can be the sign of a person who cannot find anything.

A lot of time is wasted looking for "stuff" in a law practice setting. Stuff in multiple stacks on the floor, stuff scattered on tables and credenzas, stuff under the sofa—stuff everywhere.

The practice of law by its nature is information intensive. All the information that is gathered in addressing a matter or trying a case needs to go in a place where you can access it easily and quickly and do not have to research it again or reinvent it another way.

Organization in a legal setting generally means "filing." It means getting stuff off the floor, off the table, out from underneath the sofa and into well-labeled paper files and, for emails and Internet research, into well-labeled electronic files.

If your practice setting has an established filing system, use it. If not, create your own. It doesn't matter what you *call* stuff as long as you know how to *find* stuff quickly and easily.

Too mundane for you? Don't kid yourself. It is the little stuff that will trip you up. And your supervisor or manager will not concentrate on your active mind when he or she looks at the mess in your office or when you are unable to find stuff for the scheduled call with the client. The first thought is more likely to be "What a screwup." And who needs that?

Getting organized also means paying close attention to your calendar. Many of the successful lawyers I know keep both paper and electronic calendars so that nothing falls through the cracks.

You never can be too careful when it comes to being on time and meeting deadlines. You don't want to miss the hearing or show up late for the call because it was not on your calendar.

Show Respect for the Time and Schedules of Others

And always pay extra close attention to your daily/weekly/monthly planning when that planning involves the work schedules and expectations of others. For example, if you are planning to take a vacation, do not wait until the last minute to announce that you will be out of the office for the next week while you are in Tahiti without a phone or Internet connection. Last-minute notice does not go over well with management and colleagues.

Instead, have discussions about when you would *like* to take your vacation in advance of purchasing your airline ticket and get your supervisor's approval for that timing. Supervisors often have much more information and perspective than you do about work on the horizon and tasks coming your way. Get them in the boat on your plans. (And if you don't, be sure to buy trip cancellation insurance!)

One of my contributors also points out that it is important to let colleagues know where you are and how you can be reached by using the electronic calendar and "out of office/in a meeting" functions. He knows that young lawyers often feel they need to disappear without anyone knowing it to tend to a sick child or take a work break to recharge over lunch. He also knows that all these things are essential to doing your work effectively and that everyone else has non-work commitments too. So, trust that your colleagues will understand, and let them know as soon as possible where you can be reached in an emergency.

The same contributor points out that there is nothing more frustrating from a supervisor's perspective than not knowing until two days before a brief is due that the person you need a draft from is out for the next few days. Be transparent with your availability—always.

However, he also adds a corollary to this advice. He knows that a managing lawyer should be understanding and able to work around work interruptions, ordinary vacations, and scheduled days off, and he shares this:

> "I recently heard a story from an associate about working with a partner in his firm's New York office. The associate attended a long-planned wedding and was out the Friday before for out-of-town wedding activities. In response to the associate's well-drafted out-of-office message, the partner responded, "I never have put up an out-of-office message. I am always available."

That is the wrong message for a managing lawyer to send. It does so much damage to *esprit de corps* and is so unnecessary. Power moves like this have no place in the profession.

Pay Attention to Convention—That Means Rules!

Rules, rules, rules. By now you are tired of hearing about them. But they are *so* important.

You may have colored outside the lines all of your life. Loved pushing the envelope. Enjoyed being an outlier. But now is not the time for that.

Every organization has rules. Some of them won't make sense to you in the early years of your career, and you will need to have patience with them as you continually remember that you do not have the power in those early years to change the rules.

If you want an environment with no organizational rules to stifle you, become a sole practitioner and be your own boss. There is nothing wrong with that. But learn how to practice law first from people who know how so that you are ready to handle a practice on your own.

Sociologists teach us that human beings generally desire rules, even yearn for them, because it cuts down on so much of the burdensome decision-making. So, follow that thread. Listen carefully to the rules and internalize them. Make them a part of your everyday routine, while at the same time understanding that it does not insult your independence to play by the rules.

Some of the rules involve your responsibility for entering your billing logs, which will be discussed a little later. Some of the rules have to do with Continuing Legal Education, which you *must* have to be a functioning lawyer in your organization. Some of the rules have to do with committee participation. And the list goes on and on.

Most of the rules and conventions are simple housekeeping matters, but they are very important to the successful operation of the business. For your own good and personal success, put a smile on your face and do your part.

Be Sensitive to Office Politics—and Avoid the Worst Kind

Often you will hear people say that they do not get involved in office politics. It is too risky. And that can be true. There is not much to gain by taking sides on issues that do not affect you or showing favor based on likability or popularity or position. Staying in your lane is usually the best advice.

And the kind of office politics that borders on gossip is particularly dangerous for young lawyers and can result in backlash. In dealing with those kinds of situations, think of yourself as Switzerland. Be neutral. "No comment" should be your comment.

There is nothing to be gained by getting involved in conversations about the personalities in your office or who is sleeping with whom. Gossiping involves very bad judgment and generally comes back to bite you. And you will set yourself up to be the next target of gossip.

But there are likely to be times when you feel the need to talk to someone about the "outrageous" behavior going on in the office. In that case, tell a friend—not a colleague—and leave names out of the conversation.

One of my contributors, however, has another take on office politics:

> "You don't have to be active in firm politics—especially if you do not intend to aspire to partnership. But you must at least be sensitive to firm politics because doing so will give you freedom and peace of mind when planning the rest of your life. Let's say you want to take a 10-day vacation to Puerto Rico, or you don't want to do employment litigation anymore, or that you got an assignment on Christmas Eve and are trying to

> make an informed decision about whether to blow it off or suck it up. You can't make an informed decision about any of these issues without having at least some insight into firm politics and economics/dynamics. For example, how secure is your job based on the influence of the partners you work with? Has the firm been making or losing money lately? Are you the only transactional lawyer admitted to practice in a key jurisdiction?
>
> Basically, you need to understand how much capital you have with the firm. And you can't have a full picture of that unless you are at least generally tuned into firm politics."

This is excellent advice. It puts a new face on office politics and how they can affect you and be important to your career.

But remember that everything that may seem like office politics to you, is not. For example, you may find yourself caught between two managers who both want your full attention on their projects. You can be in only one place at a time.

That is *not* office politics. That is case management, and it is above your pay grade. Let the managers have a discussion and figure it out.

Establish Work Priorities

You will find that your work starts piling up faster than you expected. Soon the honeymoon of your first law practice job is over, and you are working for multiple managers on multiple projects. It will seem overwhelming, and you will wonder how you possibly can do it all.

You need to establish priorities. Prepare a "to-do" list every night before you leave the office, check off what you get done the next day, and add new things that pop up. Revise, revise, revise, and that list will become your work plan. In executing on that work plan, one contributor cautions that you need to be prepared to work harder than your mentors. Don't be the one to point out that a senior person leaves the office every night before you do. That person was junior at one time also, and what is expected of you now was expected of him or her then.

And don't always prioritize client work over law firm housekeeping requirements. For example, remember that law firms run on what clients pay. In a law firm, the business office prepares bills based on time logs submitted by lawyers, and those bills are sent out to clients for payment. Those are known as accounts receivable. Collections of those accounts receivable are how the law firm keeps the lights on, the heat on, the doors open for business, and the employees paid. So, it is not unusual for firms to mete out penalties for late time logs—meaning that offenders get fined.

Master the Art of Billing Hours and Tracking Expenses

More specifically, the process of billing logs, draft bills and collections goes like this. Your time logs are used by the business office to prepare draft bills that are reviewed, revised, and approved by the partner, who has the most significant relationship with the client. After any revisions/additions/deletions by that "relationship partner," the business office prepares the final bill and sends it to the client—usually with a cover letter from the relationship partner.

Time logs that do not precisely explain the nature of the work performed can be a real problem, and learning to fill out time logs correctly must be a priority for you. One contributor advises this:

> "Learning to fill out time logs correctly is both an art and a science. You need to start doing it right from Day 1. There are lots of different styles and ways to craft every single time entry that you make. Get tips from partners and mentors. Your time entries are judged by the relationship partner and the client. The client will be asking, 'Am I getting my monies worth? I see a 3.5 hour entry from a young associate at $675 and hour. That calculates to $2,362.50 and the entry from the associate states that is for researching a topic. What the heck does that mean?' The next thing that happens is that the client complains about the bill and the associate, and the partner has to (1) argue with the client to justify the bill or (2) write down or write off the entry by the associate. This is not a happy result for anyone."

This gives you some insight into how partners view vague references on time logs. It causes them heartburn, to say the least. So, don't do it and be exact in your descriptions to make the time you have logged easier for the partner to explain or justify to the client. The partner will appreciate you for it—and will be much more likely to use you again.

You also should not procrastinate in filling out your time logs. Don't wait until the end of the month to reverse engineer your time. That is a nightmare. Avoid the hassle and create time logs at least once a week (from notes you take at the end of each day). At the end of the month, you will be so happy that you did.

Some lawyers think they are too busy to fill in time logs on a daily or weekly basis. They fall into the habit of keeping notes in diaries and then agonize at the end of the month to jog their memories and make some sense out of those notes from references that are too vague. Too often they end up filling in the gaps with what could be considered fiction.

It is much better to record billable time when the work is fresh in your mind than 30 days later—when you might be making some of it up. That is a very bad look for a lawyer.

It also is important to track your expenses on a regular basis. Although your assistant will take care of your travel scheduling and expenses/payment related to client work (like hotel and airline reservations) you will incur other expenses to purchase meals, take taxis and Ubers, and meet other business-related needs. Keep all your receipts and include them in your expense report for each trip. Retracing your steps on expenses is *really* time-consuming, and clients only want to pay for what is well documented.

Be aware, however, that plaintiff's firms do not bill by the hour. Plaintiff's firms typically bill on contingent fee bases that are determined from the amount of a judgment, jury award, or settlement. For example, if the representation agreement states that the law firm is entitled to one-third of what is recovered on behalf of a client in a personal injury case, that one-third will be calculated at the conclusion of the matter—whether in court or by way of settlement. However, expenses in contingent fee cases are paid on an "as incurred" basis and typically are billed to the client monthly. So the expenses have to be documented throughout the representation not just at the end.

Be Careful with Social Media

How you portray yourself to your colleagues and clients is very important to their perception of you and your future success. It includes how you talk to them, what you say about yourself to them, and what you put on Internet sites about yourself and about them. The rule of thumb is that you should not talk about the particulars of your job on your personal social media outlets.

I know that most of you have grown up with social media and that it was an enjoyable diversion for you as a teenager and young adult. There is nothing wrong with continuing that interest as long as you can be certain that it will not negatively impact your career.

The problem is that you cannot be certain that your career will not be negatively affected if you are using social media for personal reasons. Because it is not all under your control. Social media, by design, is out of your control.

And, if you believe that your supervisor will never see something that reflects badly on you or about you or about the firm because he or she is too old and clueless to access new communication networks, you may be very wrong. Most practices have people on staff who are savvy about social media as part of the firm's risk management program. It will turn up. It always does.

Rather than wait for the other shoe to drop and the questionable picture *of* you or comment *about* you or comment *by* you from a social media post to end up on your supervisor's desk, just be prudent and discreet and cut your losses. Anticipate the worst and do damage control.

And while you are thinking about this, focus on the fact that certain social media sites allow anonymous comments. You never will know who has decided to take you down, but you may be left with the exponential effects of just one nasty tweet and thousands of retweets. And you never can put that genie back in the bottle.

However, you do need to learn to use social media for business purposes to let others know what practice you are engaged in at your firm and any specialties you fulfill within that practice. Think of a LinkedIn profile, for example. The objective is to get the word out about your practice and attract clients.

Most large law firms have marketing departments that can provide guidance on professional social media postings. For example, most firms control what you put on such platforms about specific representations and require that all client-related and matter-related postings are approved by the client relationship partner.

But not all lawyers and law firms have marketing departments. Sometimes the electronic marketing falls to individual lawyers in smaller practices. So, here are some tips from a *Lawyerist.com* article titled "Should Lawyers Use Social Media?"[2]

> **How Should Lawyers Use Social Media?**
>
> Absolutely, lawyers should use social media—and for many reasons. Your clients are spending some serious time on social media. Around 3.8 billion people currently use social media. These people spend an average of 2 hours and 24 minutes on social every single day.
>
> Plus, around 54% of consumers use social media to perform research prior to making a purchase. Before a potential client decides to reach out to you, they're looking at your social media.
>
> Furthermore, 71% of consumers who have a positive experience with a business on social media will recommend the business to friends and family. Talk about the positive effects of word of mouth.
>
> These stats communicate one message: if you don't have a social media presence, you're missing

---

[2] https://lawyerist.com/marketing/social-media/.

out on critical leads and referrals for your firm. It's time to get on board.

How Not to Use Social Media for Lawyers

One of the most important lessons you can learn from this guide is how *not* to use social media as an attorney. You must practice good social media hygiene to reap its benefits and protect your reputation. Here are some things you shouldn't do.

- *Be fake.* To communicate your law firm's brand effectively, you need to be authentic. There's no need to force a voice or tone on social that isn't you. If you aren't known for being funny, avoid it. Stay true to yourself.
- *Feed the trolls.* You may receive comments from people who simply want to stir up trouble. In the social media world, we call these trolls, and it's best to ignore them. Remember, don't argue or fight online. Should you need to have a conversation, do so behind the scenes and in a civil manner.
- *Forget to apologize quickly and completely.* Should you say something you shouldn't or post something controversial, apologize quickly and completely. Mistakes are human and owning up to them will build trust between you and your audience.
- *Try to build a presence on every social media platform.* You don't need a presence on every platform. This is a surefire way to experience burnout. Choose the platforms your ideal clients use. As a beginner, it's okay to start with one channel and build up over time.

- *Use social media as a billboard instead of a place to connect.* Your social media accounts shouldn't be a billboard of promotional content. Instead, use your platforms to chat and connect with your audience. Answer their questions and alleviate their fears.

So, now you know. Proceed with caution.

Use Your Emotional Intelligence

There should not be undue emphasis on Intelligence Quotient (IQ) in our profession. Legal education programs and bar exams are very challenging, and it stands to reason that most of the lawyers at your office are quite intelligent or they would not be at your office. So, forget about IQ.

The more important kind of intelligence for business success is *emotional intelligence*. How perceptive are you about the objectives and emotions of those around you? Do you regularly ask yourself what makes people respond in a certain way or do you just hold everyone to *your* performance standards? Are you aware that there are countless things that can affect people's behaviors, and do you allow for that in the way you react to them and what you expect of them? Do you build lasting alliances based on trust? Are you fair with others in the way that you want them to be fair with you?

Think about your answers to those questions. Have your antennae up to avoid problems and remember that you are not the only one under stress and burned out. And remember that overreacting and singling others out for *their* bad behaviors can sometimes be perceived as *your* bad behavior.

Too many young lawyers become strident and outspoken about "that awful person in the office" who offended them, and they can't wait to catch the offender at it again.

They are preoccupied with evening the score, and that distraction interferes with their work and gets noticed by others—who do not want to become part of a personal vendetta.

Emotional intelligence also comes into play when dealing with authority figures on the job. Some of them do not have much emotional intelligence and they do not treat junior people very well.

But one thing they do have is rank and power. They are superior to you, and, no matter what you think of them, you need to be respectful and keep from showing attitude with them. One of my contributors has this advice: "Challenging your superiors can be a good thing in moderation, but you have to make sure that you are not only respectful but also that you are correct."

However, if it is not just a particular authority figure who is the problem but, rather, all authority figures, you need to get some help asap. Dealing with authority figures is required in most jobs, so you have to learn to do it effectively. Even solo practitioners have judges and clients who pull rank on them when it comes to decision making.

Control Your Temper

Losing your temper on the job also is a really bad look. If you know that you have a temper problem, learn to control it. If you cannot control it on your own, get help from a therapist. At some point who is right and who is wrong does not matter anymore. Leadership just wants to be rid of the problem, and that may mean getting rid of you.

And never act out of anger. There will be many times when you will be justified in feeling angry at your opponent, a judge, a colleague, or even a client. However, most lawyers find that any reaction or response born out of anger is something they come to regret. It often just leads to more frustration and complications. You should act thoughtfully and intelligently at all times.

Most of the time you should just get over your grievances and get into your work. However, in certain circumstances, that is not possible, especially with co-workers. You soon will learn that not all young co-workers are created equal. Some of them will take advantage of you. So what do you do about that?

Protect Your Work Product

You never should let another person claim ownership of your work product. It is bad enough when someone appropriates your idea at a meeting, but laying claim to your work product is wrong on a whole other level. You cannot overlook an offense like that, and, in some situations, you may have to bring it to the attention of a supervisor or manager. If that becomes necessary, make sure you are on solid ground on the facts, and do it right—respectfully, politely, and professionally.

Here is a tip from one of my contributors. He emphasizes the need to reduce all of your work product to writing. A memo to file will do. The manner in which you approach the importance of your work makes it much more difficult for someone to misappropriate your ideas and work product.

It gets even more complicated to protect your work product if the person you are complaining about happens to be a "favorite" around the office. But, even in that case, you really have no choice. If you do not point out the offense, it will continue and someone else will get credit for your work.

In both these situations, however, first get advice from someone you trust who understands the situation and knows the players. Your mentor would be a good place to start. You should not try to tackle sensitive things like this alone.

Good role models are important to this discussion. All role models, like all co-workers, are not created equal. Some are good, and some are bad. Young lawyers typically emulate behaviors they see, and sometimes the behaviors they model are unacceptable and unprofessional. Some senior lawyers get away with bad behaviors because they are responsible for huge accounts and bring in big money. However, that does not make their behaviors acceptable—it just makes people willing to accept their behaviors.

Young lawyers emulate behaviors they see, and sometimes the behaviors they model are unacceptable and unprofessional. Some senior lawyers get away with bad behaviors because they are responsible for huge accounts and bring in big money. However, that does not make their behavior acceptable—it just makes people willing to accept their behavior.

As a newbie lawyer, however, you cannot get away with bad behavior. You must be very cognizant of emotional intelligence and acceptable behaviors for those at your level of practice and experience.

If you think that bad behaviors cannot be costly, think again. Read this recent article, "In-House Counsel Out of a Job After Using Wildly Inappropriate Nicknames for Co-Workers,"[3] about a senior lawyer who lost his job because of bad behavior. You can see that it would have been easy for a junior lawyer to "play along" and join in the fun. It also would have been very costly.

---

[3] https://abovethelaw.com/2022/03/in-house-counsel-out-of-a-job-after-using-wildly-inappropriate-nicknames-for-co-workers/.

Be Respectful to the Staff

Sometimes emotional intelligence and good behaviors are as simple as knowing how to treat the people who help you do your job. Do not come off as arrogant or uncaring or you will become the talk of the break room. "Please" and "thank you" go a long way. So does a cup of special brew or a deli sandwich from time to time.

More than one contributor advised, "Be kind to *all* staff, and treat them with respect. Legal assistants, paralegals and all staff are critical to the success of every lawyer. Get to know them and learn from them. They can make your life easier or they can make your life miserable, so act accordingly."

Another contributor wrote, "Don't think you are better than anyone (because you aren't)," and yet another contributor added, "Don't act like you are entitled." And I add, don't taunt people. Don't pick on their weaknesses. Don't try to elbow them out to make room for yourself.

And don't be difficult. Another contributor points out that sometimes young lawyers think that they have to prove their toughness by being critical of or condescending to others. Here are his words:

> "No one is worse to work for than someone who is trying to prove he or she belongs by diminishing the contributions of others. Before you criticize an argument or strategy, think of a way to express it in positive terms. It might be, 'These are all good arguments, but we may be able to enhance them by looking at it from a different perspective.' People will work harder for those they trust and like. Be that person."

And help people. When someone in your office needs assistance, help them. It may be a partner, a fellow associate, or a staff member. It is a great opportunity to establish a positive reputation, and the help is usually not forgotten.

It not only is the right thing to do, but it also is likely to work in your favor when *you* need help. One of my contributors wrote back to me a second time to ask that I remind you of this: "If you are going through hell, look around and find your battle buddies. Those relationships may be among the strongest and longest lasting professional relationships you will build."

This advice was definitely worth a second email. And it made me especially grateful for the time and effort that my contributors have dedicated to your futures.

Steer Clear of Toxic People

As one of my contributors puts it, "Toxic people can be hell to deal with. And you should not have to. Do the best you can to avoid those people whenever it is possible."

I have written extensively about toxic work cultures, especially within law firms. Those negative cultures, and the leaders and managers who allow them to exist, are what drive people out. There is a saying that "people do not leave jobs, they leave managers," and I believe it. You can put up with a lot of late hours and hard work, but putting up with a manager who does not reflect your values and encourages bad behaviors is something quite different.

One of my contributors, a young lawyer himself, has this to offer:

> "As a young lawyer, you are entering a professional environment. Although everyone should act like a professional, unfortunately not everyone does. Avoid people who create a toxic, unhealthy environment. You are not obligated to put up with

unprofessional behavior and toxic environments. Move on from that environment as soon as possible. It can feel perilous, but you will thank yourself later."

I also think it is the responsibility of all lawyers to nip toxic behavior in the bud when they see it or hear it. If you see or hear a junior lawyer being dressed down openly and in a way that will cause him or her great angst and embarrassment, you are likely to feel a responsibility to tell someone. You will recognize that it is not a proper way for a senior lawyer to give feedback and that it needs to be called out. Verbal abuse never should be allowed.

As a young lawyer, however, calling out bad behavior—especially by those senior to you—creates an uncomfortable and perilous situation. However, be sure of your facts, report only what you personally heard and saw, and trust in your mentor. Share the information and let the mentor do the rest.

Set Boundaries

Establishing boundaries makes others respect those boundaries and respect you. For example, do not always be the one to take on the unwanted tasks because you need to be liked. If you do the unwanted task once, don't repeat it. Let someone else step up the next time.

Don't always be the one to volunteer to stay late. Although it can demonstrate cooperation, doing it all the time may become a burden to you and will set unreasonable expectations by others. Whatever your personal and professional boundaries are, protect them and your career.

Learning to set boundaries early in your practice on the less important stuff is a good way to start. It will prepare you for the time when, as a more senior lawyer, you need to say "no" to avoid getting overextended and stuck in the morass of a loser of a case.

So you do not want to wait until it is too late to test out your comfort level with setting boundaries. First, however, you will need to do some soul searching about what those boundaries are and how realistic they are for your situation. For example, saying that you will not work on weekends doesn't fly in most practice settings. It is unreasonable and puts client representation at risk. It will backfire on you.

And, when you are setting boundaries, don't become known as "that person" who always refuses new opportunities or new challenges. You are expected to be a team player. As one of my contributors points out,

> "You never want to be the one who seems reluctant to help out a partner who is in a pinch. You can really tarnish your reputation that way, and the partner will not come back to you the next time."

Be Confident and Watch Out for Imposter Syndrome

Law practice is often referred to as a confidence game. It is no place for doubters, and you need to be your own best advocate to get ahead.

But being confident is a lot easier said than done in a profession as demanding and competitive as the law. And it is easy to get mired down in thoughts that you will not succeed. You need to continually remind yourself that you have been successful in all that you have done leading up to your early practice years, and that this experience is likely to turn out the same.

Keep in mind, however, that the road to success is not a straight line. The majority of lawyers experience failures and disappointments and ups and downs along the way. It is not fatal to you or to your career. In fact, most lawyers will tell you that it was their biggest disappointments, and even failures, that helped them become better attorneys—as well as better human beings. As a contributor notes:

> "Have confidence in your legal education and experience. And remember that there is no "right" answer to many of the problems you are going to confront."

Another contributor puts it this way, "Persevere and have faith in yourself." He recognizes that much of the fulfillment and reward of being an attorney is "backloaded" to the time that you have developed as a mature and accomplished lawyer. He recommends that you do your best to enjoy the path to learning how to be an excellent attorney, along with all the trials and tribulations.

Be patient with yourself. Anticipate the time when you will feel the exhilaration and reward of being an accomplished attorney, one who clients and colleagues seek out and depend on for advice in the most important challenges they face.

A contributor also points out that you need to convey the confidence you have in yourself to colleagues and clients. In addition to your legal expertise, what clients are looking for is reassurance in getting through tough situations. They want whatever comfort you can reasonably give them without overselling the case or misleading them about the risks.

Be aware, however, that being overly confident with partners and clients can lead to problems. As one contributor points out:

> "It's very tempting (and often natural) to tell partners or clients things like 'I'll send you the draft by 5 pm.' However, doing so can be dangerous because it exposes you to breaking that promise, even if it's just a small promise, which is a cardinal sin of lawyering. Although most people—including lawyers—break lots of tiny promises every day, a lawyer should endeavor to limit those occurrences. It is crucial to your credibility and reliability that you only tell the truth when wearing your lawyer hat. So, instead of saying the draft will be ready by 5 pm, say 'I intend to send the draft back by 5 pm' or 'I expect to be finished with the draft by about 5 pm.' In other words, under-promise and over-perform."

A low level of confidence is difficult to deal with. Imposter Syndrome is even worse. If you did not experience Imposter Syndrome in law school, you were lucky to escape it. Count your blessings.

Some of you may remember sitting in class and hearing another student give a completely remarkable cold-call answer. Your reaction was to doubt that you ever could sound that brilliant. It suddenly became all about you.

That is Imposter Syndrome, and it rears its ugly head in law practice as well. The root cause of Imposter Syndrome is the feeling "Why am I here? This place is full of much more accomplished persons, and I can't compete with them." Although the syndrome is often identified with women in male-dominated and testosterone-driven workplaces, it also happens to men.

Maybe you already have experienced it in the law practice setting. Think about times when you offered an idea or participated in a conversation during a business meeting, and someone in the room disagreed with you. You immediately thought that the contrary opinion made you look less intelligent and less competent.

The only effective way to overcome Imposter Syndrome is to value yourself, your background, and your achievements. It is all about self-confidence. As the name indicates, self-confidence comes from *you*.

Start by reminding yourself that you are in the room. You are at the firm. You are in the courtroom. You got there because you are competent and others have confidence in you. Now it is your turn to have confidence in yourself. And remember, if you do not have confidence in yourself, it will be hard to convince colleagues and clients to have confidence in you and your expertise.

If you turn a blind eye to all that you bring to the table, and if you are reluctant to advertise what one contributor refers to as "your value add" at every opportunity, your self-confidence will be vulnerable to erosion. And you will become a prime candidate for Imposter Syndrome.

I remember having feelings of insecurity as a young lawyer. I replayed every conversation I had with colleagues in the hallway and every word I uttered at a hearing to make sure that I had not sounded like a fool. And sometimes I was unable to convince myself of that because speaking in some environments, and especially before a judge, can be very stressful. And then I had to fight very hard to regain my sense of self-confidence.

Don't even go through that kind of Monday morning quarterbacking because you are worthy of more. Instead, chalk it up to experience and know that almost every lawyer you know or ever will know has similar stories of self-doubt. It is part of the learning curve.

However, as one contributor points out, "Don't oversell yourself either. There is a lot to learn, and that is OK. You have time."

Be Flexible

The practice of law is changing so fast these days in both substantive areas and the way legal services are delivered. The enhanced pace of practice to meet client expectations in a very competitive legal services environment can make your head swim, but you need to be prepared to embrace change in a positive and meaningful way. Being flexible is one of the ways you will survive.

Professional flexibility can mean changing your expectations to meet the needs of others. Specifically, it can mean being willing to change a meeting time if possible, reshuffling work responsibilities to meet the needs of the team, or volunteering to take a meeting when someone else is "slammed." In other words, being flexible means being cooperative, which is very important when you are building your brand both inside and outside the office.

The concept of flexibility with colleagues and on behalf of the organization is front and center today as part of the larger debate about working from home. It is framed by issues related to the isolation during COVID-19, but it looks like it will outlast the pandemic.

Working from home during the pandemic was especially difficult for lawyer-mothers and other primary caretakers without help in their homes, but some lawyers found working from home enjoyable and comforting. Many of them were young lawyers who did not experience the concurrent and overlapping burdens of combined family responsibilities and law practice, and they enjoyed the convenience of working from home. As a result, many of them have been especially reluctant to return to the office.

Now that law employers are calling employees back to offices, young lawyers need to understand how their lack of flexibility on that issue can impact their professional futures. I often hear, "I never will go back. I have been very productive while working from home, and they won't make me return." That may be unrealistic. It is all about who has power over you and what their objectives are.

Managers know that young lawyers need face time with supervisors and positive role models to develop critical practice skills and to become familiar to others within the organization. Without those interactions, young lawyers run the risk of being easily forgotten.

A supervisor is much more likely to remember your face and your name after he sits across the room from you during a meeting and observes you. Your supervisor may ask you a bit about yourself when you have finished a meeting with her and are headed out the door. That one-on-one exchange gives you the opportunity for a little casual chit chat that helps fill out your profile and makes you less forgettable.

Building rapport is very important in a law practice setting, and it is a whole lot easier in person. There is little time for casual conversation during a meeting on Zoom. And, when the host leaves the Zoom meeting, you leave too.

Being in the office and experiencing face time also is the only way you can get a real sense of what effective lawyering is all about. It is where you observe the subtleties of positive communication skills, good meeting skills, good mentoring skills, and successful conflict resolution skills. It is where you learn what it takes to develop new work, and it is where you are most likely to meet a client. If your only experience with a client is on Zoom, you better hope for a very good connection and a sharp focus. Technology is not perfect.

Managers also know that events like summer associate programs to entice new lawyers to the practice and client events depend on the in-person presence of more experienced lawyers. The participation of experienced lawyers assures the opportunity to build connections to the next generation and convince them to join the firm, and clients want to see their lawyers at events. If experienced lawyers do not return to the office, those opportunities may be lost.

As noted in a recent *Above the Law* column, "Habits are formed and a lot of people have gotten very comfortable working remotely. They've gotten into a routine, and that routine offers a lot of things, like cost savings."[4]

That is an important concept. Those cost savings include the cost of transportation, the cost of clothing appropriate for the office, and the cost of additional childcare. The timing of these inflationary pressures are big issues for some lawyers, and those considerations are worthy of discussion in the debate about in-office presence versus working from home.

But if your reluctance to return to the office centers solely on your continuing desire to work in sweats all day or hang out with the dog, those are not good reasons for refusing to return to the office at least part of the time. Decisions like this fall under the heading of being prudent and protecting your professional future.

Also keep in mind that your managers and supervisors can be very "old school." They are used to traditional office structures, and, post-pandemic, they will be hard to convert to full-time working from home models. And I remind you again that they are writing the rules. Until you break into management, you need to consider how balking at the rules can impact you.

However, I also am aware that the legal profession is currently experiencing an associate hiring frenzy in some large firm transactional practices especially, and firms have been hiring with the understanding that exclusive working

---

[4] https://abovethelaw.com/2022/04/biglaw-leaders-realizing-theyve-got-no-leverage-when-it-comes-to-making-lawyers-return-to-the-office/.

from home will be allowed. Although it may appear that the rules have changed, in reality those accommodations typically are for a select group of lawyers who service a unique market. And whether the demand in that market will last is unknown at this time. In fact, as this book goes to print, it is reported that the most profitable law firm in the world, Kirkland & Ellis, is starting to lay off associates in its corporate practices due to a slowdown in those practice areas. What this means for other law firms and the future of the profession is uncertain.[5]

I also am aware that there are other exceptions to the face time preference at law firms. Senior associates, who have demonstrated value and started the upward climb to partnership, may be in a different position and able to be more creative with working from home. Their managers have developed confidence and trust in them over time, and, even though face time is still important for them, it is not as important as it is for entry-level lawyers.

Another issue that you need to remain flexible on is promotion. While it is true that most lawyers want to advance upward in an organization, it can become an obsession. Be flexible and do not let that happen.

Keep in mind that the pathway "up" is different for different lawyers. Sometimes it depends on class year, and sometimes it depends on practice group needs and considerations. Not all firms promote on "lockstep" basis, which depends on associate class year, and your firm may be one of them. Or your firm may have promoted by lockstep at one time and now has a different policy that makes the path to promotion less certain.

---

[5] https://abovethelaw.com/2022/11/stealth-layoffs-arrive-at-worlds-richest-biglaw-firm/.

The most important thing to enhance your probabilities for promotion is to do the best job possible in a way that makes people notice. As one contributor points out, "Don't worry constantly about or ask a lot of questions about when or how you will make partner." That is likely to annoy and irritate the very people who make the promotion decisions.

So, play your cards right. Choose to be flexible on issues like face time, working from home, promotion decisions, and other matters that are closely aligned with the professional perceptions you create. I once was told by a boss that perceptions can be as powerful as facts. I believe it, and you should too.

Show Enthusiasm for Your Work

Showing enthusiasm for your work is very important. The impression of enthusiasm you create will go a long way toward having you embraced as part of the team.

When a manager or supervisor sends you *one more assignment*, accept it with enthusiasm. If you are able to pull it off, that strategy will lead to your personal power through the confidence and loyalty you build up with your superiors. It will help you in charting your own positive career course, including the future ability to credibly turn down projects that are not of interest to you.

But being enthusiastic and meaning it are not always possible, and being blindly enthusiastic can be foolish. If you have so much work on your plate that you doubt whether you can meet existing deadlines *and* take on new work, you must bring this to the attention of the one requesting the new work. Explain exactly what your deadlines are and your concerns. As a contributor has written, "Say yes as often as possible, but get comfortable saying 'no' when you must."

And, if you need further help resolving the workload conflict, bring in another supervisor or a mentor to help work it out. No one wants you to be so overworked that you cannot produce quality work, and some things are above your pay grade and out of your control.

Another contributor has this sage advice:

> "Don't worry about what you cannot control. Just understand what is expected of you and do your best—that is what you can control. Worrying about what you cannot control takes your focus off what you can control."

Be a Valuable and Effective Team Member

The team concept that once was reserved for sports and business settings, and included in most MBA curricula, has become just as important in the law practices of today. So, becoming a valuable and effective team player is critically important to your success.

The qualities of a good teammate include loyalty, reliability, openness to new ideas, and being around until the job is done. Good teammates work on behalf of each other. They respect each other. They meet their deadlines to the team. They are adaptable. They are cooperative, and they venture outside their comfort zones when it is necessary.

And they have mission clarity. That means that, if you have a question about the approach to an issue or what has to be done in response to an assignment, you do an email to other team members to clarify your approach and responsibilities to the team.

You need to put the team's needs ahead of your own and not complain about the inconvenience. As noted in an edition of the *Law Career Fitness Challenge* blog, it is important to make sure your personal needs do not get in the way of what the team is trying to accomplish. Team leaders are aware of who is not carrying his or her weight and responsibility to the team. Be sure that you are not one of those people, and as noted by one of my contributors, "Don't be a martyr about it." Complaining will not gain you sympathy with others who are doing their share to get the job done.

Being positive is also important as a team player. There are a variety of opinions on a team, and only one chosen strategy. Your opinion is not always going to prevail, and positive team players don't sit around and pout if they do not get their way. They accept the decision of the team and cheer on their teammates.

A number of my contributors have identified a sense of humor as very valuable in a team member. Laughter can be an important factor in relieving pressure and reminding teammates that you are all "in it" together. You may not be the superstar on your team, but your sense of humor will be valued.

Another team quality that is very important as tensions mount and deadlines lurk is the ability to avoid "freaking out" and creating crises that do not exist. That kind of emotional breakdown or catharsis is not helpful to anyone and can be a major distraction.

And one of my contributors, a managing lawyer, reminds me to tell you that being a good team player also means being thorough. In particular, he points out that you must "read the attachments" to a supervisor's memo before speaking to the supervisor about the work. He says that nothing is more frustrating than setting up a call to discuss documents and hearing on the other end, "I just read your email summary but haven't had time to review the underlying document." The only option then is to reschedule the call to avoid wasting a lot of time.

Another important aspect of being an effective team member is to use team players correctly. As pointed out by one contributor, your assistant/paralegal is there to help you. Even though associates have learned to "do it all" with the downsizing of administrative ranks, things like scheduling videoconferences, booking meeting rooms, and processing expenses are routine tasks that are better handled by assistants or paralegals.

Delegating those responsibilities will pay dividends by making the assistant/paralegal feel more like a part of the team, and young lawyers, who learn to delegate effectively, will acquire managerial skills like team building, leadership, and loyalty. Those skills will prove invaluable when the time comes for them to manage a complex case.

And a final bit of advice from a contributor is that you never ask a team member to do something you wouldn't do or at a time you wouldn't do it. An example would be setting a deadline for a weekend day—when you typically don't work weekends. Or if you have not worked after 6 pm all year, don't ask for a draft by 8 pm. The person you ask knows you won't read it, and your insincerity will be noticed by others as well.

Perhaps the most effective way to be a valuable team player is to make yourself indispensable. One contributor explains it this way:

> "Be proficient with technology, like PDF editing/redacting, using fax machines, filing on CM/ECF. Many partners run up against deadlines all of the time and are completely befuddled by modern technology. If you can rescue them from fast-approaching deadlines with your expertise in simple computer functions, you will cement yourself as an indispensable asset. Make the partners rely on you."

Don't Allow Others to Marginalize You

The need for self-confidence was addressed earlier in these strategies. However, it is important that you remember that the confidence you have in yourself is not *all* under your control. You can be undercut by others who will try to marginalize you. Be on the alert for that and nip it in the bud.

We all have experienced it. It may take place at a meeting where another lawyer overlooks your contribution as unimportant and unworthy. It may be in the break room when someone belittles you for your performance. Or it may be at a firm event when someone makes a joke at your expense. If it continues to happen, you need to confront it.

You need to call it out with a bit of humor and with a smile, and, if possible, you need to recruit a colleague to call it out also. For a woman who is being marginalized by a male, recruiting a male colleague for support can be very effective.

And *never* allow yourself to be marginalized for the entertainment or personal gain of others. Managers and supervisors should be on the lookout for this kind of bad behavior, but they are not always paying attention. So, you need to look out for yourself.

Here is how it worked in White House staff meetings during a recent administration, as reported in mainstream media after the fact. It was reported that some women staffers were being cut off during their remarks by male colleagues or were having their ideas co-opted by those same colleagues. So, the women adopted what came to be known as "amplification." When a man repeated what had already been stated by a woman, another woman would make it clear that the same thing had been offered by a woman earlier. And it was noticed by POTUS, who then called the women into his office and asked for an explanation. The women described what had become the marginalizing habits of the male staffers, and POTUS said that he would take care of it. And he did.

In following staff meetings, the President called on the women staffers more often and encouraged their participation. Sometimes it was his gentle reminder that one of the female staffers had made that exact point earlier, and sometimes it was a good-natured admonishment to curtail interruption and allow the speaker to finish her thought. Whatever it was, it worked. Good leaders know how to change bad behaviors.[6]

Ask the Question You Are Afraid to Ask

Never be afraid to ask a question. *Never* be afraid to ask for clarification.

This is a real problem for many young lawyers. They are reluctant to go into a senior lawyer's office to ask a question. They choose to spin their tires looking for an answer on their own rather than chance "looking stupid" in front of a supervisor.

That is a big mistake. First of all, as an entry-level lawyer, you are not expected to know all the answers. You have very little experience and expecting so much of yourself makes no sense.

Do not worry about whether your question is a good one or a bad one or whether your analysis of the issue is right or wrong. Just get your thoughts organized and ask the question.

Consider the alternative. If you decide not to ask the question and chase some ill-conceived notion down a rabbit

---

[6] *See* "The Amazing Tool That Women in the White House Used to Fight Gender Bias" (Sept. 14, 2016), https://www.vox.com/2016/9/14/12914370/white-house-obama-women-gender-bias-amplification.

hole, you risk being in real trouble with your supervisor and with the client. Do damage control. Ask the question.

Here is some great advice from one of my contributors, a young partner who is not so far removed from where you are now. He starts at the beginning—with your understanding of what is being asked of you:

> "Whether it is a lawyer receiving instructions from a client or a junior lawyer receiving instructions from a senior lawyer, it is easy to be overwhelmed by a flurry of instructions and to get 'lost in the weeds.' Take the time to relax, sit back and absorb what you think the request is. Take time to better understand the task, and, if you still are not certain after that, develop follow-up questions to discuss with the requestor."

That is totally consistent with my own view of this problem. I have supervised young lawyers enough to know that the last thing I want them to do is sit in their offices in states of perplexed wonder because they feel uncomfortable approaching me with a question. And I know other supervisors feel the same way too.

In private practice, particularly, managers do not want lawyers billing extra time on issues that can be easily explained by someone who has encountered those issues and situations before. Those managers do not want to be in the position of cutting billed time just because a young lawyer was afraid to ask a question.

That does not mean that you always will get the clarification you need. Sometimes you won't. Some managers are too busy, and some of them don't care about your practice development. They just want what they want when they want it.

The truth is that, in toxic workplaces especially, it can become a kind of sport to hide the ball and make junior lawyers pay their initiation dues by figuring things out for themselves. Once when I discovered that a partner had information that he had not shared with me and that caused me hours and hours of time to discover on my own and I confronted him about it, he responded that I had not asked him the exact right question. Clearly it was a game with him. He thought that he was toughening me up before trial.

This was wrong, of course, but it still takes place. To think that it will go away any time soon is not very realistic. Some senior lawyers do not have any desire to make anything easier for you than it was for them.

So, sometimes you may just have to go it alone and hope for the best. And, if that is where you find yourself, do not overlook the value of senior associates who likely have encountered the issue themselves. They can be very valuable to your skill development.

Even if you think you understand the task, getting clarification can be especially important when you have been briefed verbally on a new project. It can be hard to engage with the briefer and take good notes at the same time. To be sure that you are not missing something or are not going in a wrong direction, send an email after the briefing stating what you understand the assignment to be and ask for confirmation or clarification. You also may want to ask for rough estimates of the number of hours you should spend on the assignment. Do not assume that supervisors want a full memo on every issue. Sometimes they do, and sometimes they are looking for something less. It is much better to know in advance.

Here is how one of my contributors, a supervising lawyer, puts it:

> "Always be sure that you set expectations. As a manager, I don't always remember to tell you when I need something done. I'm moving to the next

call/meeting/crisis. Make sure you ask me what work product I am asking for and when I need it. Remind me that there may be others in the review chain before we can file something (a client, interested party, investor, paralegal for example) and that we may need to back the deadline up accordingly. We may need to revise the entire timeline after thinking about this."

You can save yourself a lot of time and agony by just asking a question. And it is a very easy thing to do.

And then you will not be hopelessly down the rabbit hole!

Work Smart and Seek Out Help When You Need It

Sometimes your needs related to work assignments will go beyond clarification. You will be lost in the weeds, and you will be tempted to push that project to the bottom of your "to-do" list because you just can't figure it out.

Procrastination is a waste of time, and wasted time is your enemy. As a young lawyer, who is relied on to get the job done within the expectation of supervising lawyers and clients, you must become as efficient as possible. That means being a good time manager—and being a good time manager means confronting the issue.

Work smart and get the help you need. Working smart means asking for help whenever you need it and especially when you are confused. You can become confused about how best to approach an assignment, how to make contact with opposing counsel, how to prepare for a deposition, how to structure a transactional document, how to file a document with the court, and the list goes on and on and on. And you must be able to work yourself out of these quandaries to reduce the stress caused by being confused.

You will find that most lawyers are happy to get you moving in the right direction and on the right road. Senior lawyers and even associates more senior to you are both good sources of this kind of information—because they all have been in your situation. If you run into one who does not fit that description, reach further. Help is out there.

Knowing when you need help is something that most of your colleagues will respect. Just don't become a bother. Don't ask for help before you try very hard to figure it out for yourself. But when you reach the point where you are just spinning your wheels, it is time to pick the brain of a more senior lawyer. Working smart means knowing when to bring in a second or third opinion.

As a contributor notes, "Working smart also means going for answers and solutions and not just identifying problems and challenges. Partners and clients want solutions not law school 'could be this or could be that.'" Another contributor puts it another way: "Clients, in particular, do not like being told 'on the one hand this, and on the other hand that.' They want one-handed lawyers."

Working smart also means not being afraid to ask for work that stretches you and forces you to take risks to gain experience. The response may be "no, because you are not qualified yet" but at least you asked the question. That kind of initiative can be very impressive to managers and supervisors.

Find Effective Mentors and Sponsors

Effective mentors and sponsors are important in private practice, in-house, government, and other practice settings, and they can make the difference between success and failure. They have the potential to enhance your career across a practice setting, and you need to identify them, build those relationships, and invest in them as counselors and guides.

You should not limit your search for sponsors and mentors to your own gender. Women and men very often differ in practice styles, and those differences can become important to you. Experience with differing approaches will broaden your perspectives and make you a better lawyer.

Knowing the difference between mentors and sponsors is also very important. Although they overlap in terms of discipline and purpose, they perform different functions.

Mentors teach you. Some law firms have mentoring programs that assign associates to more senior lawyers. I am not a fan of those programs because they typically do not take personalities into account. Too often, the matches are based on common experiences, like being from the same region of the country or graduating from the same law school.

In my experience, an organic process is better and more productive. Allowing an associate to identify a mentor, who the associate feels comfortable with, has a rapport with, and whose judgment the associate trusts is an example of this process. Ideally, the mentee and mentor should share a practice specialty to provide the best teaching/learning experience, but that is not always necessary.

Hopefully, there is someone assigned to the mentoring program in your practice setting who can work with you to find a mentor that suits you. Such a program leader should recognize that it is too much to ask most entry-level associates to approach senior lawyers requesting to be mentored, and, if that is expected, many mentee–mentor relationships will never get off the ground. It is better and much more comfortable for the program leader to assume that role and move the relationship forward.

If you find that the mentor that is either assigned to you or chosen by you is not working well, be sure to talk to the program leader about it. The solution does not have to be to terminate that mentor relationship, which could have complications for you, but to add another more effective mentor. It is not rocket science, and the objective of having a good mentor–mentee relationship is beneficial to both you and to the firm. Your professional development is an asset that the firm needs to protect, and mentoring is very important to that process.

In choosing a mentor, also do not discount the value of senior associates. Typically, in large firms the best mentors are the associates who have gone through what more junior lawyers are experiencing and can give excellent advice and guidance. They can help you through difficult times, and they know the value of providing that help because someone helped them along the way.

Effective mentoring can include periodic meetings or lunches for catch up and discussion of what you are working on and next steps. Mentors can teach you about substantive aspects of the law, and they also can answer your questions about the way the firm works and who does what. They also can be sounding boards for problems you may encounter in navigating the organizational system, and how best to resolve those problems.

A good mentor listens to you, is interested in what you are saying, and is not dismissive. He or she gives useful advice and keeps bringing the conversation back to core themes to enhance your career. A good mentor also puts you at ease and does not think any question is silly or inappropriate.

Additionally, one of my contributors has this excellent parting caveat about mentors:

> "Be careful that you do not become too closely identified with your mentor. If your mentor

"screws up," you are gone, too. You also need to be careful not to get too comfortable with a mentor, losing your ability to work with other partners when necessary or to think for yourself."

Good to remember.

Sponsors, however, have different roles. They are typically partners in your practice area, and their role is to help you with strategy related to your advancement, and, when it comes time for promotion, to advocate for you.

Sponsors keep their eyes out for professional opportunities for you, they guide your career, and they put themselves and their professional reputations on the line for you. A sponsor is typically someone who you have impressed with your work and who is willing to take a chance on supporting you.

Finding a sponsor or a mentor does not happen on Day One. You need to have patience and take an active role in selecting those who will be so instrumental in your career. You need to keep in mind the "style" that you want as a practicing lawyer and avoid mentors who represent behaviors that you do not embrace.

For example, if you are a litigator, you don't necessarily have to be what one of my contributors, a litigator himself, calls a "bulldog." And if you don't want to become a bulldog, you also don't want a mentor who is a bulldog. My contributor points out that there are very effective litigators who approach litigation matters with finesse and subtlety, and he recommends finding a mentor who fits your style and who speaks your language.

But sometimes the process just does not work. One of the greatest disappointments over my practice career and now as a career consultant has been witnessing the reluctance of some senior women lawyers to mentor younger women lawyers. When I was a young associate, there were very few senior women lawyers to act as mentors—and there were none in my firm. But that is not true today. Today there is a significant increase in the number of senior women lawyers, but, unfortunately, not all of them are willing to mentor younger women.

These senior women typically are not supportive of things like flexible hours and maternity leave because they did not have those programs available to them, and they do not think they are necessary. Some of them also enjoy their experiences as one of very few women in management positions, and they are not ready to welcome more women into that exclusive club.

I have few patience with those uncooperative and unsupportive attitudes. I believe that all women lawyers should be supportive of all other deserving women lawyers. It is still a tough climb for women, and "paying it forward" should be something that senior women are willing to do and want to embrace. Women who started practicing 30 and 40 years ago should be pleased about the advances that women have made in the profession—not resentful.

Years ago, the *Wall Street Journal* included an article titled "The Tyranny of the Queen Bee." Here is an excerpt.

> "This generation of queen bees is no less determined to secure their hard-won places as alpha females. Far from nurturing the growth of younger female talent, they push aside possible competitors by chipping away at their self-confidence or undermining their professional standing. It is a trend thick with irony: The very women who have complained for decades about unequal treatment now perpetuate many of the same problems by turning on their own."

And just recently, *Harvard Business Review* explored this same issue in an article titled "Research: How Bias Against

Women Persists in Female-Dominated Workplaces,"[7] where the situations in law firms were explored at length. So, unfortunately, the problem continues.

This can be a big problem for young women lawyers, and the only silver lining is that many of the Queen Bees already have retired or are close to retirement. Their uncooperative attitudes will not be missed.

As the recently departed former Secretary of State Madeleine Albright once said, "There is a place reserved in hell for women who do not help other women." I had the pleasure of meeting Secretary Albright and discussing those words with her. She completely understood the importance of that quotation to women in the law profession. She was a pioneer for so many professional women through her prescience and example and support, and she will be missed by so many.

If you find yourself in a setting where senior people cannot or will not serve as role models or act as mentors, you may feel like you are on your own in terms of developing a practice style. In that case, you will need to look outside your organization to associations and groups to find suitable role models and mentors. Watch what they are doing to advance their careers and how they develop business. Incorporate the best of what you see into your own personal brand.

And, if you are not finding the cooperation you need within your firm, start thinking about whether you are in the right practice setting. There may be a better place for you and your talent.

[7] https://hbr.org/2022/03/research-how-bias-against-women-persists-in-female-dominated-workplaces.

Pursue Feedback on Completed Assignments

Asking for feedback on your work is very, very important, and it is critical to a positive learning experience. But it can be challenging. First, it may require you to be very proactive. And second, you must be ready to hear some things that may be hard for you to hear.

One of my contributors points out that lawyers are very bad at giving feedback and that, while you are being proactive, you need to be careful that you are not being irritating and annoying. He has this tip from the time when he was a newbie lawyer:

> "After I would submit my work product for a senior lawyer to review (a pleading, a letter or a contract, for example), I would check the file a few days later to see what had been sent to the client. I would do a blackline comparison to see what changes the senior lawyer had made to my original submission to him. In those cases where I saw that I went wrong or if I had some questions about specific changes, I would bring the blackline to the lawyer and talk about the changes."

That is excellent advice and recognizes the responsibility of associates in settings where senior lawyers often are very busy. Because of the competing interests in their practices, senior lawyers do not always take time to get back to junior lawyers about their work products. It is not necessarily that they don't care. More often it is a function of time and availability. So, you need to seek them out and ask for a post-project review.

And sometimes you will discover a discrepancy in the billings that will alert you to an issue and make it clear that such a discussion is necessary. For example, on matters that are billed by the hour, associates often have access to their monthly billings and equivalents in cash collected from clients for their work. If you see hours you worked and reported that have not been billed to the client or a reduction in cash received from the client for your work, that should be an indicator that a conversation with the billing partner is warranted.

And when you finally have the opportunity for that conversation, be a good listener, embrace constructive criticism, ask follow-up questions, and don't be defensive. Accept it as the important learning experience it is intended to be. Then apply the lessons learned to your future work.

This last part is often difficult for young lawyers today. In many cases, they have met with a lot of praise and accomplishment in their lives, and accepting criticism is not easy for them.

The best thing you can do for yourself in this situation is to *expect* criticism. Even if it does not come your way, you might ask how you could have improved on your work product. This is your time to get inside a seasoned practitioner's brain and pick it a little for your own benefit.

And it is not just the work product that can be improved by constructive criticism. When you take constructive criticism well and put it to work on your next project, you also are improving your self-confidence.

Keep in mind, however, as pointed out earlier, that improving your self-confidence does not mean that you should become delusional about your abilities. You need to identify not only your strengths but also your weaknesses and how to overcome them. One of my contributors suggests that you can learn a lot about your strengths and weaknesses by taking a Myers-Briggs personality test and use what you learn there to embrace/capitalize on strengths and consider areas that need improvement. I know some of you may shy away from those tests, but you need to use all the resources available to you.

Recently I spoke to a young lawyer who had a particularly difficult evidentiary hearing in federal court and was lamenting her performance and the judge's response to her arguments. I reminded her that she never had handled that kind of hearing before—and with such a difficult witness—and, basically, what did she expect?

One of my young contributors points out that entry-level lawyers face a steep learning curve in a rather unforgiving environment. He adds that:

> "They know that everyone has extremely high expectations of them. But given their inexperience and the pace of the work, young lawyers are bound to make a few mistakes along the way. Recognize that not every mistake is career-ending and, in fact, few really are. The key is to recognize the mistake, acknowledge it, and show your team that you have a suggestion for a solution. Handling mistakes gracefully and addressing them with solutions is an important life skill and much appreciated by colleagues."

Most lawyers can recall moments of vulnerability when they were forced to hear things that they did not want to hear. But they also can remember moments of elation and empowerment at having overcome that doubt and put a difficult chapter behind them. As one of my contributors puts it:

> "Asking for feedback includes the inherent admission that you're not perfect. But constructive feedback will make you more perfect if you treat it seriously."

Another mistake I hear about too often is young lawyers hiding behind impersonal technology when asking for feedback. They choose email and texting over in-person conversations. That is a big mistake.

Be brave. Be bold. Face the music. Ask for an in-person meeting where you are able to ask follow-up questions and get the most out of the feedback.

And, once you have the feedback, remember that feedback in that context is subjective. Also remember why you asked for it.

Forget about whether you like the person who delivered the feedback or whether you think it was fair or accurate. Let it mull around in your brain a little to gain some maturity and to help you get over what might be disappointment and resentment.

In most cases, you will conclude that there was some merit to the feedback—for the simple reason that it will have come from a more experienced lawyer. And it is your job to identify that merit and use it to improve your future work products.

I never will forget when I was a newbie lawyer and having a partner—very demonstrably and in a VERY loud voice—say to me, "Don't you ever . . ." And I never did that thing again! He turned out to be one of the most effective mentors I ever had, and we are still in touch today. Part of what I became as a lawyer was because of him. I knew he had my best interests at heart.

Zoom Well

You need to understand the culture of Zoom. It may seem silly to you, but more than one seasoned attorney has gotten into trouble on Zoom.

Zoom—and other competitors in the virtual meeting market—are here to stay. The technology became essential during the pandemic and proved to be a viable alternative to in-person meetings, and almost everyone in the business world today views it as a necessary convenience. The platforms are so popular and prevalent these days that it would not be surprising for you to be in a Zoom session on Day One for a training session. So, here are some Zoom rules.

Do not appear on Zoom looking like a cat.[8] And do not have inappropriate virtual backgrounds.

Do not eat during the session. But, if you must—because of your busy schedule or your desperate need for nutrition—absolutely do not talk with your mouth full.

Try not to have kids and animals running in and out of the session. However, those unexpected events at times may be uncontrollable.

Be fully dressed and pay attention to the camera angle and what other participants may see. Lack of attention to this has done serious damage to at least one very high-powered lawyer. In "When Zoom Goes Boom! Top 5 Zoom Call Disasters—Ranked,"[9] you will read about the worst of the lot.

Zoom also is challenging in terms of having free-flowing conversations. You need to wait your turn to talk, and interruptions become problematic. You can use the "chat" box, but that often seems stilted and lacks spontaneity. So, your emotional intelligence must be engaged at all times during Zoom calls. And that can get really exhausting.

In all things Zoom, keep it professional and tasteful.

---

[8] If you have not seen the video of the lawyer appearing before a judge behind a cat-faced filter, here it is: https://www.youtube.com/watch?v=lGOofzZOyl8.

[9] https://medium.com/the-haven/when-zoom-goes-boom-top-5-zoom-call-disasters-ranked-fd94257858c7.

Become Competent at Self-Advocacy, Networking, and Business Development

Self-advocacy and networking/business development really draw on the same skills. If there is any difference, it is that you advocate for yourself within your organization by representing your interests to be assigned quality work and leadership positions, but you network and develop business outside your organization to get new clients.

Self-advocacy is essential to success in law. If you wait for others to recognize your talents, it is often too late or it may never happen. Colleagues and supervising lawyers may be too busy to come to you. So, you need to make your talents apparent to them.

One of my contributors describes it this way:

> "Make yourself known (but not in an obnoxious way). Lawyers are notoriously bad delegators, so it is very important for a young lawyer to be proactive about getting the type of work he or she wants. If you are interested in a certain area of practice, seek out an experienced lawyer in that field and ask to help."

The same proactivity is required for effective networking and business development outside your firm, but the target of your efforts is prospective clients in the business community and within your personal contacts. And the payoff is new clients that create autonomy in your practice and portable work that you can take with you to another practice setting.

To be successful in both self-advocacy and networking/business development, you must be willing to *ask for the work*. Typically, you are not going to *get* the work unless you make it obvious that you *want* the work. And your "ask" will have to make a case for why you are the best person for the job.

It may help you to think of networking and business development as an extension of good communications skills. It requires you to identify what relationships you want to foster and what promotional and networking settings are most comfortable for you. It can be lunch with a colleague, meetings at professional associations, or interactions with people at your kid's school, in your place of worship, or at your exercise club.

Networking and business development also can include public speaking and writing articles. Although that sounds intimidating, it is very valuable in improving your communication skills and increasing your visibility both inside and outside your organization.

Law firms should be paying more attention to teaching all young lawyers to promote themselves in the firm and to network in the business community. Firms also should be providing venues that give young lawyers opportunities to test their skills.

When I supervised young lawyers, I challenged them to demonstrate their networking skills in business settings like bar association and industry meetings and professional conferences. The morning following the event, we would meet in my office to discuss the contacts they had made. They would bring the business cards they had collected, and we would talk about strategies for future connections.

I always asked the young lawyers what they talked about with those new contacts. Sports and the season's best movie alone were never good answers. Although finding a common ground of interest is important as a conversation starter, effective networking eventually needs to come around to you and your business.

Although it is optimal to have a champion to introduce you to potential clients you would like to meet, the truth is that often you need to figure networking out for yourself and develop your own style. Here are some suggestions to get you started.

Set the Foundation

Establish some procedures. Decide that you are going to take a potential client to lunch one day of every month or that you are going to attend two networking opportunities each month. Stick to the schedule, and you will be surprised how much easier it gets.

Also, have a good "elevator speech." Here's what that means.

The term "elevator speech" is a fictional reference to the time it takes to get from the tenth floor of a building to the lobby in an elevator. If it takes two minutes, then your elevator speech should last two minutes, and the location can be anywhere. It is not limited to an elevator.

Your elevator speech may begin in response to a polite inquiry from a stranger in line with you at the deli—as in, "Do you work around here?" Your answer should include where you work and what you do. "Yeah, I work in a law firm around the corner" works and does not have to include your position or the name of your firm. If a business network is meant to develop, that will be enough and it may be all the time you have. Hope that you see that person again, in that same line, to further the conversation.

Or you may seize the opportunity and introduce yourself to a perfect stranger at your child's school and start a conversation. Asking what the other person does is a good way to begin because people like to talk about themselves.

Sometimes the answer takes more time than you have, so always have a business card ready as a backup. "Here is my card. I would love to continue this conversation. Give me a call" is a good way to encourage further contact.

Most elevator speeches should start with a description of your practice in one sentence. For example, "I am a trial lawyer, and I specialize in fraud litigation involving government contractors." Contrast that to simply saying you are a lawyer. Follow up with a brief description of your firm, as in "I am with XYZ, a firm of 200 lawyers that specializes in . . ." And *always* offer your business card—which you should keep in a place that is easily accessible. If you find yourself fumbling around in your briefcase or bag for a card, the opportunity may be lost.

A good elevator speech is not just for newcomers to the profession. Every practitioner must continue to hone his or her elevator speech as career goals and practices change.

But effective networking does not end with the elevator speech. Sending a follow-up email or text is very important. Also add the contact to your mailing lists and, if your business has a newsletter, add your new contacts to that list as well.

Another useful follow-up is to periodically send your new contact any materials that you think will be of interest. It can be a new agency ruling that affects his or her business, a media article of interest, a judicial or jury decision, or information about an upcoming conference or program. Always include a short note.

Follow Up and Have Patience

You can do these things over and over without much response. But then one day your phone might ring or your email might ping, and it could be your lucky day.

To be successful at self-advocacy and networking/business development, you need to stop thinking of it as a chore or as something that only super aggressive and annoying people do. Telling people what you do and how well you do it is providing them with valuable information that not only may be important to your career development but also could be important to their businesses.

So, think of it as doing them a favor. If the person walks away or is not responsive, there are two possibilities: either that person is very rude or your elevator speech needs improvement. You can't do anything about rude people, but you can work on your elevator speech.

Another good venue for networking and business development is to join a board of directors that your firm will support. You will meet peers and potential sponsors who can prove very valuable to your career. But be careful not to overcommit.

You will be very surprised that even young lawyers are needed on many not-for-profit boards of directors. I have served on a variety of those boards, and I know the value of young and enthusiastic voices in those settings.

Also be aware that networking is not limited to professional contacts. You also should network with your personal contacts. Although your law firm may stress professional marketing and business development, a very important source of future work and opportunities will come from your network of professional and personal friends. Finding clients among them also will provide a great deal of independence.

To do that, it is important that you stay in touch with your friends and acquaintances, other lawyers in your network, and undergraduate and law school classmates, who can be the source of future referrals. Check in with them from time to time and let them know that you are following their careers and progress. And they will follow yours.

A contributor notes that the more seeds of friendship you sow, the better your career and your life will be. He says that it is the healthiest way to practice and live. And you may find that some of those contacts—not all of them—will grow into valuable client relationships as well as friendships.

Hone Your Negotiation Skills

Negotiating for yourself and self-advocacy are related concepts. If you learn to negotiate effectively for yourself, you also will be able to negotiate effectively for your clients. So, there is a double benefit.

The purpose of negotiations is to resolve something in your favor. So, it could be negotiating for a higher salary or better benefits. It could be negotiating for a reduced schedule or a flexible schedule. It could be negotiating for a bigger office or a larger role in a case. It could be negotiating for a transfer to another branch office.

Negotiating for yourself can be tricky because it typically involves things that are very important to you.

When negotiating for yourself, keep the following in mind:

- Be prepared with facts/research to support what you are asking for and be calm and in control of yourself.
- Adopt a communal win-win style in your delivery to send the message that what is good for you is also good for your employer.
- Listen to other opinions and positions to show respect.
- Be open to a reasonable compromise.
- Expect pushback and accept it with a smile.

- Adopt a gentle and friendly manner and avoid appearing intractable.
- Make eye contact and assume an open body posture to show approachability and poise under pressure.
- Argue your "case" without an excess of emotion in the same way that you would argue on behalf of a client.
- Be yourself. If aggressive is not your personality, don't try to fake it. You can be assertive, persuasive, and compelling in ways that do not require you to be aggressive.
- Know your value and don't apologize for your requests and positions.
- Be pleasant and maintain a sense of humor.

Your goal should be to present yourself as competent and likable, powerful and inclusive. You want to get the upper hand without being offensive.

Choose to Be a Leader

You should choose to be a leader at every opportunity. Leadership is founded on being the best at what you do and earning the trust and respect of your colleagues. It most often comes from thoughtful, inclusive, and cooperative behavior and advice, transparent communication, and consensus building.

You need to start small as an associate, but there are leadership opportunities everywhere. Volunteer for jobs at the office that others do not want. Remember that nothing is "beneath" you, but also remember that there is a fine line between being cooperative and allowing others to take advantage of your good nature.

Get involved in committees at your practice and in outside settings like bar associations. Your efforts will be noticed, and it is good training for the future leadership opportunities that come with promotions.

Whether internally in your firm or in external organizations, joining and participating will pay huge dividends. Meeting people and making yourself known will be advantageous to you and will signal that you are prepared to invest in your career beyond just your legal skills. That kind of investment is what partners do all the time, and it is good training for those skills as you advance in the firm.

You also can be a leader in your community (as discussed again later in this book) and in other non-professional settings. Find a cause that you support and join it. It can lead to valuable expertise and leadership positions that your firm and your community will respect.

The more opportunities to lead that you experience, the more effective a leader you will become. Although successful leaders are often thought about in the context of making difficult decisions and giving orders, they also build consensus and delegate effectively. And those are often their greatest contributions.

One of my contributors reminds you how important it is to delegate. "Learn to delegate. Embrace synergies and leverage. This applies both at work and in your personal life."

That is a very good point. Trying to do it all yourself does not work well in a profession as demanding as the law.

Learn Law Firm Economics

Every young lawyer needs to become familiar with law firm economics. The more you know about the business model of the law firm, the better you will understand the roles of your supervisors and other senior lawyers and the pressures on them. This knowledge will make you a more empathetic colleague.

Specifically, you need to understand "overhead," which is a fancy name for expenses that are necessary to keep the wheels of the business rolling. And you also need to understand how revenues (the proceeds collected from clients) are allocated. If you understand these concepts and how they define your role in the organization, you will be light years ahead of many other entry-level lawyers.

Expenses are easy to understand. They include rent, heat, electricity, furnishings, equipment, supplies, services, costs of events, and the like. Expenses also include salaries of managers, who are not timekeepers, and salaries of non-equity partners and employees. Think of expenses as everything that is necessary to keep the doors open, the lights on, and the office buzzing with clients and worker bees.

But "allocation of revenues," which includes determining salaries, is more difficult to understand. The short course is that most law firms, and particularly those that bill by the hour, use some variation of the 1/3-1/3-1/3 approach to allocation of revenues.

According to that formula, one-third of the total potential revenue earned *from your work* goes to *your salary*. Another third goes to pay expenses (overhead), and one-third becomes profits that are distributed to equity partners. That profit distribution to partners from revenues gained from the work of associates is what "leveraging" means in law firm parlance, and it is based on the concept that partners are rewarded with profits for taking the risks of decision-making and bringing in new business.

This is a general rule, and you should want to know whether it holds true in your firm or whether another formula applies. You will discover that by showing interest in firm economics and asking your mentor or another trusted supervisor about it, you will feel like you are part of the business.

But not on Day One. That is a little too ambitious. Wait until you have developed a trust relationship with a mentor, and then inquire about the economics of the firm. A good mentor will tell you what you need to know.

In all conversations make it clear that you are not asking for proprietary information that is available only to partners and managers. You just want a basic primer on how the organization runs and your role in making it a successful business

It also would benefit you to know what kind of financial support you can get from the firm for the purpose of networking and marketing. Although partners typically have what amount to expense accounts for those purposes, associates typically do not. But you may find that there is money to support networking and marketing efforts by associates in a firm client development account or comparable fund. You will never know unless you ask, and you will be showing real initiative and savvy by asking.

Show Initiative and Act Like an Owner

Another way to show initiative as an associate lawyer is to approach your assignments as if you "own" the work—in other words, as if you are the partner in charge. Although you are not a true owner of work until you generate it, you can "act" like an owner. And it will be noticed.

Acting like an owner assumes that the job/assignment is yours until you hear otherwise. It means not only following up on assignments after you have submitted them but also checking back to offer help on next steps. Acting like an owner enhances your leadership skills and creates the perception of you as very valuable to the organization.

That approach will make you think like the client is yours, and, by all means, you do not want to lose a client. The sooner you start to think that way, in terms of analysis, strategies, and client relationships, the more valuable you become to the firm.

One of my contributors gives this advice:

> "Regularly reassess the situation presented by every case or matter and don't be afraid to approach your supervisor/manager/partner and suggest that it may be time to change course. New facts come to light all of the time that affect strategies and advice, and you need to be willing to respond and not be held back by your prior assessments."

This is excellent advice, but I caution you to be careful how you have those discussions with superiors. Making suggestions and asking your supervisor/manager/partner whether you are on the right track is usually a good idea, and most of them will welcome the initiative. However, all of them are not likely to be as open-minded and receptive as others. You will know right away whether your suggestions are welcomed. If they are not welcomed, let it go. If one supervisor/manager/partner does not appreciate that kind of initiative, others will.

And as another contributor points out, "Never upstage the partner." When you are in the presence of the client and the partner, *never* contradict the partner or try to put the focus on yourself. It is incredibly dangerous.

It is easy to remember this if you think of it in this way: The partners are your clients too. Whenever I hear young lawyers say that they have never met a client, I remind them of this. The partner is your client.

A contributor agrees with me and points out:

> "You always must make the partners happy because they are your clients. Typically, servicing the client well will make your partners happy. As a junior associate, your ultimate objective is to make your partners' lives easier."

Thinking like an owner is the best preparation you can have for becoming one. For example, when I was a partner supervising junior lawyers, I always welcomed their initiative. We would work together on a first case, and I would prepare the outline of work, including the workflow, the deadlines, and the issues to be researched and briefed. I would provide as much input and feedback as possible to increase the value of the learning experience.

But when the second case came along, we would reverse roles. I would tell the associate to act like the case was his or hers. I expected the associate to prepare the outline of work, monitor the progress of the case, review all of the research, and make sure that we were meeting every deadline.

I knew that it was intimidating for associates to assume that kind of case management responsibility, and I acknowledged that to them. But I also knew it was the best training they could get and that they knew I was in their corner. And in the end, I was always gratified to see how much that approach raised their confidence levels and how much more valuable they were to me and to the firm because of that experience.

Another contributor points out the value of knowing your client's industry in acting like an owner. He says that it is essential to learn as much about your client's work/industry as possible and that clients want you to care about their businesses—not just their legal work. If that involves reading industry-related news and publications, do it, and ask clients questions about their work. Showing that you care about their business and the big picture is important to them and pays dividends to you.

This advice is echoed by another contributor, a particularly seasoned litigator. He says that one of the most enjoyable things about his work is learning about what clients do and becoming a mini-expert on that work to represent the client well. As a commercial litigator, who represents clients in a variety of industries, he looks forward to the next representation, what he can learn from it, and how he can apply that knowledge to future experiences.

Plan Your Career Early and Often

The profession of law will not naturally unfold to meet all your needs. You must plan early and often as your circumstances change and opportunities arise.

Effective career planning means thinking about what you want your career to look like five or ten years down the road. In other words, what are your career objectives and where do you want to end up? Do you want to be a partner in a law firm or do you want your experience to take you in a different direction? How do you define success? Knowing those answers makes the journey a lot easier.

If you want to be a law firm partner or a person of power in another legal setting, a lot of responsibility for whether you reach that goal falls on you. All jobs have requirements for advancement and promotion and taking the position that the requirements are unfair is not a winning argument. If you advance to leadership in an organization, then you will be in a position to change those requirements. Until then, you are held to them.

There are enough variations in practice settings to meet your needs if you try hard enough to find them. And there are myriad other opportunities outside law practice—some which might appeal to you and fit you better.

Always remember, however, that leaving practice and re-entering at a later time is very challenging. Even though there are excellent programs today like the OnRamp Fellowship, which matches law firms with re-entering practitioners, those programs can accommodate only a relatively small number of lawyers each year. For those who are not chosen for those programs, it is tough slogging to get back into the business.

Most recently, however, individual law firms are getting active in recruiting within this market. Reuters reported in February 2022 that Freshfields Bruckhaus Deringer has developed a "Returners" program, open to lawyers who have left the profession for two or more years, whether to raise a family, take care of a family member, or to pursue another opportunity. Although it is widely acknowledged that this program is related to a shortage of qualified lawyers to handle all of the work in this very active legal market, the model is likely to be parroted in other similar programs across the industry. No matter what the objectives for these programs, they represent progress in creating opportunities for departed lawyers reentering the profession.

Pay Attention to Work-Life Balance

Drum roll, here. This is really important to your professional satisfaction and success.

Your career plan must include a realistic view of work-life balance. The profession of law is demanding and includes responsibilities for people's businesses, freedom, and futures. It can eat you up with its stresses and complexities, so you need to find a way to relieve stress and create balance in your life. Without a work-life balance that is satisfactory for you, you could find yourself in trouble that can get out of control.

In truth, work-life balance is no balance at all. At best, it is a snapshot in time—a transitory thing that is here today, gone tomorrow and substituted with another set of facts. It is measured over time and not on a short- term basis. It needs constant attention and a flexible approach.

Like any balance, it includes trying to keep everything working together to avoid a crash. Remember when you were a child and learned to ride the see-saw at the playground? It was fun, but keeping yourself from falling off required your total concentration. The balance you face today includes things that are far more complicated than something found on a playground, but it requires the same degree of vigilance.

Work-life balance is essential as a counterweight to the stress of law practice, the toxicity of some workplaces, the requirements of various practice settings and specialties, and the demands of clients, opposing counsel, and courts. And finding ways to deal with stress effectively is imperative to having a successful and satisfying career.

Although the subject of work-life balance has been associated most often with women and childcare responsibilities in the past, it is important for both male and female lawyers. In fact, with men's particular vulnerability to heart disease caused by stress and the life expectancy of men lower than for women, it can be argued that men need work-life balance and relief from stresses every bit as much or more than women.

Work-life balance can be found in spending time with friends and family, in pursuing hobbies and activities, or in simply walking on the beach or in the woods. It is not important what you do to achieve the balance, it is important that you do it.

All young lawyers should start thinking about the challenges presented by work-life balance long before they encounter them. *With the proper amount of foresight and planning, they will not be blindsided at some future time by unexpected circumstances.*

Those challenges also can include caretaking for aging family members. Many lawyers find themselves "sandwiched" between these responsibilities, and careful planning is the only thing that helps them survive the pressures.

Nothing is static when it comes to caring for families, and your planning must anticipate changed circumstances and include back-up plans. For example, don't count on your baby's nanny—even the best one who is like family to you—lasting forever. Just as others change jobs, so do nannies. You need to have a contingency plan.

The discussions about the work-life challenges for young families should include all those who provide any significant degree of childcare. That particularly applies to spouses and mates, who must be brought into the conversation and may be counted on to step up and provide a portion of the day-to-day support in the home. Sharing of responsibilities is key in this modern age to allow both mothers and fathers to prosper equally in their chosen careers.

And the pandemic was a game changer. Women lawyers surely were among those who left the profession during the pandemic because quality childcare was not available during the threat from COVID-19 when daycare centers and schools were closed. Although many legal commenters identified very high attrition rates for women lawyers due to these circumstances, I was very pleased to see one the most reliable legal commenters help to set the record straight recently.

In making her case against the oft-repeated narrative that, when push comes to shove, women bail out of their careers, Vivia Chen of *Bloomberg News* cited the most recent statistics supporting the conclusion that women remained in the workforce during the pandemic and stayed on their jobs, as much as they could, and persevered. And, citing additional statistics to show that those in the most privileged positions were able to keep their careers open, Ms. Chen concluded that most female lawyers "stayed in the game." They may have left large firms for a downsized version that afforded more flexibility or transitioned within the profession, but they did not leave in large numbers.[10]

Indeed, there are challenges. But young lawyers should not let their career planning be derailed by those challenges. Young lawyers are smart and capable of protecting both their personal and professional goals, and the advent of programs like flexible hours, working from home, and changing law practice cultures are giving them the additional help they need. Outside of another pandemic, it all should be possible. Not easy, but possible.

Flexible schedules have been especially meaningful and helpful for lawyers with childcare responsibilities. Because of flexible schedules, many lawyers are able to work from home during the hours that their children sleep and be free for family responsibilities when their children are awake. Many young lawyers, for example, go back to their home offices to continue their work after their children have gone to bed and work for hours at the end of the night. And they wake up with their children early the next morning and get them fed and off to school before resuming their professional responsibilities. They make their billable hours, and they are contributing members of their teams.

---

[10] For more on "'She-Cession' Myth Busted: Women Didn't Quit Law During Pandemic," read it at https://news.bloomberglaw.com/business-and-practice/she-cession-myth-busted-women-didnt-quit-law-during-pandemic.

As a result, there no longer is much need for part-time practice, which derailed upward mobility in the past and proved unsatisfactory and inequitable for most women lawyers. Part-time practice for them meant working full time and being paid only a portion of full-time salary.

Flexible schedules work best once children enter preschool or kindergarten, but it is more complicated for parents of infants and toddlers. It is possible, however, if parents share the caretaking responsibilities or if another caretaker can help with childcare responsibilities.

Young lawyers, both mothers and fathers, are stepping up to the plate on these issues today. I see it everywhere. They are handling the balance well and continuing their careers full speed ahead. I am impressed with their stories.

And, as a result of these advances to address issues of work-life balance, I approach the work-life issues differently today than I did in my 2012 *New Balance* book. Young women lawyers and their male counterparts are less in need of a full-blown primer on work-life balance because they have discovered it on their own at warp speed. But the types of resources available and the profiles of lawyers, who successfully faced work-life issues, in that book are still very helpful in addressing the issues.

Today, I also see a lasting need for continued emphasis on what I always have referred to as "Personal Definitions of Success," which address how lawyers view their accomplishments. Those definitions are particularly important if and when they need to step off partnership track or address alternative schedules/practice settings or transition careers either temporarily or permanently. When that happens, attitudes about professional value and self-worth can suffer, and the result is often a blow to confidence.

Under those circumstances, it is important to emphasize the unique conditions that lead to those decisions and the reality that there is no single definition of success. Success has many faces, and it is the *personal definitions of success* that dignify the choices many lawyers are required to make at some points in their careers.

So, get started early in addressing work-life balance and contemplating your choices. Don't wait until decision time is upon you and you are overwhelmed. Address the possibilities in advance and at a time when you are able to discuss them rationally and unemotionally with the others in your life who will be affected by those decisions.

That may be the greatest of all survival strategies.

Get a Grip on Your Wellness

The legal profession is demanding and rigorous and taking care of yourself, both your body and your mind, is essential to your success. As one of my contributors points out, "Make it a priority because no one is going to do it for you. Employers and colleagues can say a lot of supportive things, but, in the end, it is up to you to care for yourself."

Another contributor observes that your career is not a marathon and you need to pace yourself and pay attention to your personal needs.

> "Technical proficiency is important (and will come with time, study, and practice), but it alone is not a magic formula for career success. Give yourself permission to invest time in at least a couple of outside activities you truly enjoy (like a parent playdate group, a church group, a hiking group, a beer brewers group, a finance group—the possibilities are endless). That will not only be good for your wellness but it will help you to build authentic relationships with the added benefit of getting your

> name out and building a network for referrals. So it is a win-win."

"Wellness" echoes some of the themes of work-life balance. Increasing personal time, caring for your health, maintaining friendships, and being true to who and what you are and what makes you happy all are important to your wellness.

Wellness has been in the news a lot recently, and it is being recognized and promoted at most business organizations today, including within law practice settings. It is a recognition that, if the lives of employees and members become "unwell," the business will be impacted and things can spin out of control very fast.

The goal of wellness is to find the personal harmony that is most authentic for you. The concepts addressed by wellness include social connectedness, exercise, nutrition, sleep, and mindfulness, and concentrating on wellness means improving your life socially, emotionally, physically, intellectually, occupationally, financially, and spiritually. How individuals do that may differ, but the need to do it is becoming universally accepted.

Wellness does not exist in a vacuum and cannot be achieved passively. It requires active awareness, acceptance, and commitment. One person may need to take an expensive vacation to relax while another person can meditate. One person may require an emotional release through an artistic experience while another person can gain that same experience and value from watching a spectacular sunrise. One person may need a calm and tranquil workplace while another person can work efficiently in the midst of turmoil.

One approach is not preferable to another. The important thing is that you recognize what you need to achieve wellness and strive for it.

This is not always easy for lawyers. Many lawyers are reluctant to admit that they need help with *anything* personal—until the walls come tumbling down and they become addicted to alcohol and controlled substances and see their marriages and families fall apart. Other lawyers are perfectionists and demand more of themselves than they can deliver. Learning to say "no" is an important aspect of wellness for those lawyers.

Another important discussion of wellness centers on the importance of protecting and maintaining friendships and family relationships no matter how busy you become in your professional life. Friends and family ground you, keep you on a straight and narrow course, and give you perspective. Friends and family nurture you, rejoice in your successes, and help you through your losses. Without your friends and family, you risk ceasing to be who you really are and who you were meant to be.

Your family will always be your family, but you need to make time for your friends if you want your friendships to last. That is not always easy in a demanding profession like the law. Sometimes keeping a golf date or attending the neighborhood picnic may not be possible because the senior partner or the agency head is breathing down your neck for yet another revision or draft. However, it is important that you throw your friendships a lifeline often enough to make your friends know how important they are to you.

One contributor looks at your wellness[11] through the eyes of a manager. He says:

> "Do not neglect your well-being. Work is exactly that—work. Law is a stressful occupation,

[11] For further information on wellness, here is a helpful website: https://www.wm.edu/offices/wellness/about/eight-dimensions/index.php.

and, as a manager, I don't want your judgment clouded because you haven't eaten since lunch yesterday and only got 4 hours sleep. These things not only cause concern about the quality of the work, but they also make me wonder about your time management skills."

Stay Away from Romantic Relationships at the Office

One of my young contributors makes this excellent point: "Making friends with colleagues is one thing, and is encouraged, but romantic relationships rarely end well and can jeopardize your career."

Most lawyers, who have practiced for a while, know about office romances gone awry. And they understand that, when that happens, it is the party with the most power who is blamed the least, regardless of the facts. So, there is not much for a newbie lawyer to gain in these scenarios.

The temptation is to say, "Just don't do it." But many of us are familiar with office romances between lawyers of different power levels which have succeeded and have flourished. So that admonition seems too simplistic and too broad.

As a result, I am opting for, "Be careful getting romantically involved with someone at the office." It can be very complicated.

Do Not Tolerate Discrimination

Discrimination and biases based on gender, race, ethnicity, and lifestyle have no place in the legal profession. Although these kinds of discriminatory patterns are against the law, they can be very hard to prove. So, they persist.

Keep your eyes open, and do not allow attitudes of discrimination and even unintentional bias to short circuit your opportunities. If you think it is happening to you, talk to someone about it. If the human resources department of your organization does not take it seriously, talk to someone outside the organization.

Lesser offenses fall into the category of lost opportunities. Inequities, like not being given your rightful share of business generation or not sharing equitably in fee credits based on discrimination and bias or not being given the assignments you deserve, can seriously impact careers. You do not have to worry about some of those things as young lawyers, but they may raise their ugly heads some time in your future. Understand them now so that you will recognize them later.

I always tell my female mentees and female members of my audiences to *look out* for discrimination and bias but not to *go looking for* discrimination and bias. In other words, *be a discriminating listener but do not listen for discrimination.* There is a big difference.

Some opportunities will come to you because you *are* a woman, which is exactly what happened to me as a very newbie lawyer when my firm represented the manufacturer of feminine hygiene products in the first Toxic Shock Syndrome case tried in Federal Court in this country. To my astonishment, I was placed on the trial team. I had very little trial experience at that time, but that is not why I was chosen. I was chosen because I was *not* a man.

My primary job was to take the depositions and handle the cross-examination at trial of the female plaintiff and her chief witness, her mother. It was a jury trial, and the perception of male lawyers beating up on female witnesses was one that the firm and the client were not willing to risk. So, I was the answer to their dilemma, and it was one of the most exciting and interesting cases of my career. Everything I learned in that experience was invaluable to my future development as a lawyer.

Sometimes gender can work in your favor, so be careful where you push back. As my favorite constitutional law professor was wont to say, don't throw the baby out with the bathwater!

Practice Civil Discourse and Behave Professionally

At one time, respect and decency and honorable behavior were givens in the law profession. This no longer is true today. A fever of disrespect and indecency has seeped into our society and institutions, and it is infecting the legal profession. The manifestations of this fever are name-calling, derision, intimidation, bullying, distortion of the truth, and a lack of caring about the welfare of others. Too many lawyers have abandoned their professional responsibilities and become part of a broader societal problem. Some call it "cancel culture" and some call it just plain wrong.

Civil discourse especially has declined in recent years in the law profession. Lawyers relish in disagreement and abusive and unprofessional language to describe colleagues, parties to disputes, opposing counsel, and others who do not agree with them, and willingness to compromise seems to be at an all-time low.

I have been writing about decency and its importance to the honorable practice of law for almost a decade. Never, however, has that subject seemed more important and relevant to me than it does today. My 2020 *ABA Journal* monthly column "The Power of Decency in the Legal Profession"[12]

---

[12] https://www.abajournal.com/columns/article/the-power-of-decency-in-the-legal-profession.

includes an expanded discussion of this endemic problem, and my earlier 2016 article in *Corporate Counsel* magazine addressed the toxicity of the law profession that existed then and carries over in many legal settings today.

Civility should be the goal for all lawyers. It is important that we emulate respect, dignity, and civil discourse in our disagreements and debates because the public is watching and judging our profession by our behavior and conduct.

It is incumbent that you, the youngest lawyers today, do not behave in ways that damage and undermine the profession. Be decent. Be honorable. Be professional.

One of my contributors, an ethics expert, provided this excellent advice in a recent edition of his law firm's newsletter. In response to a report about a young woman lawyer behaving badly in a bar, disrobing, and being arrested, the contributor noted:

> "One thing I always say in these situations is you're a lawyer 24 hours a day, seven days a week. Lawyers need to be aware that whether you're in an argument with someone at a restaurant, drunk at a bar, or driving under the influence, if it winds up with an arrest, you're going to have to face the bar and disciplinary procedures."

In other words, as a professional, there is no free lunch from your bad behavior. If law enforcement does not get you, public perception will.

Live Within Your Means

If you want to have flexibility to change jobs—or even professions—and take advantage of unforeseen opportunities, you need to live within your means to keep your options open. To safeguard that flexibility, do not allow yourself to get overextended in terms of mortgages and other indebtedness that will curtail your ability to take a professional opportunity that may pay less but will be much more satisfying for you.

One of my contributors puts it this way: "Save and invest. And try to avoid lifestyle creep. Building financial security provides you career options down the line, and options are powerful."

Dependence on a private-sector salary to fuel your lifestyle has been referred to as law firm "golden handcuffs" for a very good reason. It benefits an employer who wants you to be financially constrained so that you and your talent cannot walk out the door. Do not allow that kind of constraint to limit your possibilities for professional satisfaction and success.

Also remember that starter homes are very expensive today and can require two incomes to support the purchase or the mortgage. For those of you who desire to have children, keep in mind that costs like school tuition, summer camp fees, and other wish list items can add up very fast. Always be thoughtful about your lifestyle choices so that you will be able to achieve your most important goals.

Consider a Career/Life Coach

At some point in your career, you may want to consider a career coach or a life coach. You may need a fresh and different perspective than you are able to get from mentors, sponsors, friends, and family members. There are some things that involve the combination of your personal life and your professional life that you can only entrust to an outsider with experience in the profession and objectivity.

It may surprise you to find out that many CEOs and other super achievers in business and law use career coaches and life coaches. They have them on speed dial because the need for counseling and a fresh perspective never ends. The decision to access that kind of help is an investment in your career.

I am personally familiar with Marshall Goldsmith, who is a superstar career coach, and who was my mentor when I was enrolled in coaching certification at the Indiana University Marshall Goldsmith Leadership Development and Executive Coaching Academy. My book for law firm leaders, *Top-Down Leadership for Women Lawyers*, includes extensive discussion of his teachings, and you also can Google him to get up-to-date information and read about his most recent books.

Marshall Goldsmith's clients include Masters of the Universe and Fortune 500 CEOs. The stories that he tells about these leaders—without using names or positions, of course—are eye-opening. Their vulnerability and transparency is revealing and make it clear that *everybody* can use new perspectives from a neutral party when it comes to issues about career and life. Marshall says that they are all leaders, who had the *potential for leadership* that needed to be teased out of them. He circles the globe multiple times each year to dish out his very effective brand of leadership training to do just that.

So do not hesitate to ask an expert—when and if you need it. Be assured that people at the top are doing it on a regular basis. And don't worry about perceptions. There is no shame in trying to become better at what you do and improve the quality of your life.

You can find information about coaches on the Internet and from advertisements in bar association magazines. And, fortunately, in this day of Zoom, you no longer are limited to coaches in your geographic area. Most of them have free consultation sessions, so give it a try if you need it.

Serve Your Community

All valuable career-enhancing experience does not happen at the office. One of the components of a satisfying and successful law career is service to community. Although lawyering largely consists of negotiating deals, trying cases, and improving the lives of clients and members of our society, that is just the *job*. *Being* a lawyer is more than a job. It is a *profession*, it is a *way of life*, and our professional lives should include using our talents as volunteers to reach out to those in need within our communities where the expertise of lawyers are appreciated and needed. And sometimes it can lead you to a satisfying job that you never imagined.

In my early years of practice, I was a member of the Citizens Association board in my community. At the time, I knew little about local regulations and ordinances, which dictate allowed uses for land, but I was interested in protecting my community from overdevelopment. Years later, after I had small children and was looking for more flexibility in practice, that community experience led me to a position in public service as Chief of Staff/Legislative Aide for an elected official. And that job turned out to be one of the most interesting and satisfying of my career. The expertise that I developed in that community service also led me to a partnership in one of the most respected land use law firms in my geographic area.

There are many ways of doing community service. I have served on both community boards and not-for-profit boards, and I have played an important role in raising financial support for one of the East Coast's most comprehensive help centers for women and children. And today I serve on the board of directors of a conservation trust which protects open space through perpetual conservation easements and assists in combatting the effects of overdevelopment and climate change.

My husband established the first Explorer Scout Law Program for intercity high schoolers in DC years ago and supported that program through his law firm. And, as a veteran, he also has dedicated thousands of hours of *pro bono* work to support veterans and assure that they receive the benefits they are entitled to and need.

Our stories are not unique and are echoed by so many other lawyers throughout communities, and most of them will tell you that lawyers are effective at community service because of their skills as lawyers, and they become better lawyers because they participate in community service. I whole-heartedly agree.

Chapter Three

Think About Transitions

My message in this book is not that you *should* have become a lawyer or that you *should not* have become a lawyer. All I can tell you is that you should not make that decision without getting the facts and understanding the profession. You should not decide whether the profession is for you without giving it a chance. You have far too much invested for a knee-jerk reaction like that.

However, no book like this would be complete without acknowledging the number of young lawyers who may be in the wrong business or the wrong practice. For them, even mastering the survival strategies and the core practice skills in their current practices may not be enough.

The harsh reality is that some young lawyers went to law school for the wrong reasons. Not all of them chose the career because they had deep desires to work in the legal profession.

As noted in "Should I Go To Law School? Reasons For and Against,"[1] which addresses the pros and cons of attending law school, some lawyers just fell into it. They had family members, who were lawyers, and they thought it was

[1] https://www.indeed.com/career-advice/career-development/should-i-go-to-law-school.

expected of them. It is hard to resist the lure of a grandfather, father, or mother who is a lawyer, especially when you cannot think of anything else to do after college or university graduation. Filling out the family tree with yet another lawyer seems to be the answer.

And that suggests a second very bad reason why some students choose law school—because it is a default decision. Those who chose law school by default may be the ones you saw running up and down college dormitory halls asking for opinions about whether they should take the LSAT on the eve of the registration deadline. They are the ones who may have applied to law school just days before that deadline because they had no real yen for it and had put it off until the last minute.

Another reason that some chose law school, as pointed out in "10 Good Reasons to Go to Law School (and 5 Terrible Reasons!),"[2] is that they like to argue. That is a very bad reason for pursuing a law career because most lawyers spend very little time arguing for a living, and the kind of arguing they do is not for sport. Rather, they spend most of their time reading, analyzing, preparing memoranda, dealing out legal opinions, and trolling for clients. Arguing is most often not at the top of their "to-do" lists.

Others viewed law school as an intellectual pursuit. They were unable to put the brainiac elitist within them aside—the part that craved the Socratic Method—and could not resist the lure of law school.

And even others chose law school because they wanted to make a lot of money. Although it is true that many lawyers *do* make a lot of money, even the lure of big money cannot assure happiness and contentment for most lawyers. There is

---

[2] https://studyplaces.com/10-good-reasons-to-go-to-law-school-and-5-bad/.

usually some other important reason behind those decisions. So, if money is the prime reason for choosing a career in the law, it might require further personal discovery.

These kinds of ill-advised approaches to a career in the law often cannot sustain a young lawyer when confronted with the extreme demands of law practice. Those approaches generally lack the personal passion necessary to bear down with the effort that is required to get the job done under difficult and demanding circumstances. So, it is predictable that some of you will start thinking about transitions at some point in your careers.

However, just thinking about career transitions can be exhausting. You need to take it one step at a time and not start too soon. And take it slow. Make good decisions. Do not overreact to isolated incidents that do not define you or the profession. And, if and when the time comes when you start thinking seriously about changing either your practice setting or your career, you will know where to find the information and help you need.

Do Not Settle for Less

A career is a long time. As life expectancy figures increase, so do the expectations for longer work lives. There is plenty of time for you to get career choices right.

The most important thing is that you give yourself permission to make changes that lead to satisfying and successful professional lives. To do that, you cannot be afraid of change. In fact, you need to welcome it as part of the process of becoming what you want to be.

Many members of my generation are very uncomfortable with change. The Baby Boomer generation and Generation X include too many discontented and uninspired lawyers who were too afraid to question their choices and embrace change. Dissatisfaction with their professional lives led to broken marriages, serious health conditions, drug and alcohol dependencies, and other unfortunate ends.

I am happy to report that is not what I see from young lawyers today. As I travel to far corners of the country to meet with and advise young lawyers, I see introspective and brave young professionals who are questioning their choices and looking at opportunities that are more consistent with their life goals. I see young lawyers who are struggling to find the right fit for themselves in this profession, and I see young lawyers who are looking beyond the profession.

They change jobs, and some of them change careers. They go from private practice to government service and sometimes back again. They explore myriad possibilities, and they keep their lifestyles in check to give them the opportunities to make those explorations.

I am pleased that they are not content to settle for less. They want more, and they are willing to fight for it, and they have helped create a very dynamic profession of lawyers on the move. Along the way, these young lawyers also are helping to open the eyes of management and leadership about the quality of life both inside and outside the practice.

Sometimes, no matter how hard you try, you just cannot find the right fit. It may be due to work-life imbalance, or it may be that the subject matter of your practice or your practice setting does not interest or inspire you. Or it may be that you just don't like the practice of law. Stuff happens. Lives change. You need to be resilient.

There are so many unanticipated circumstances in the course of a career, and you must be prepared for them and willing to map out new pathways to success. Whatever you choose as a definition of success, it must work for *you*.

There is no set menu for transitioning. It is a function of your imagination, your desires, your flexibility, and your ability to be realistic. Knowing who you are and finding time to protect that identity and create happiness and satisfaction in your life while billing 2,000 hours a year at a law firm may be a bridge too far, and you need to know when you have reached the end of that road.

Transitions require taking risks, and it is not for the timid. Transitions can be excellent adventures, but they must include good information and good choices. Do your homework. Read and research. Ask questions. Craft solutions. Consult with people who have made similar transitions and learn from them. Find out what their mistakes were and try not to repeat them.

Keep on questioning and keep on perfecting your personal brand. Strive hard to satisfy both your professional and personal needs out of respect for yourself.

And if you need help along the way, get it. Do not be shy about asking. Become active in your local bar association where you will meet lawyers in varied practices who have had experiences that may be instructive to you and who may be able to lead you to opportunities that fit you well. Talk to people outside the profession about their career paths. Find a coach that suits you. Nothing should be off the table.

I know some of you who have risked it all and transitioned careers. Some of you have taken incredible chances and used up your savings to do it. Some of you have found practice settings and practice specialties that were not attractive to you at first but have come to fit you very well. And some of you have left the profession and never looked back.

One of my mentees left a law firm to become a chocolatier and later returned to in-house practice. Another left private practice to start a business helping women re-enter the workplace after childbirth. Another transitioned from practicing lawyer to become an executive search firm consultant.

And I have heard and read many stories of others. They are the pioneers in our profession today.

If you find yourself contemplating transitions within the practice of law, I have included information below about the variety of practice settings and practice specialties. And the Internet is full of testimonials from lawyers who made the kinds of transitions that you may contemplate in the future.

And if you have tried and cannot be happy practicing law, start looking outside the profession. That information is also included here. Staying in will just make you more unhappy, and your unhappiness will affect all aspects of your life. If you cannot be good for yourself, you will not be good for anyone else—especially the ones you love.

In that case it is not giving up. It is *getting up* to new possibilities.

An article on Above the Law dated March 8, 2022, is instructive here. The article by Wendi Weiner titled "How to Write a Resume for a Career Outside of Law (and More Alternative Careers to Consider)"[3] is one of a number of articles Ms. Weiner has written for Above the Law about transitions, both within and beyond law practice. Her contact information is included at the end of the article.

An Overview of Law Practice Settings, Specialties, and Related Careers

Let's make sure that you have a good overview of choice of practices and law specialties to help make your transition decisions easier. It may be that you jumped into one kind

---

[3] https://abovethelaw.com/2022/03/how-to-write-a-resume-for-a-career-outside-of-law-and-more-alternative-careers-to-consider/.

of practice setting without understanding the choices, and, in that case, the following information could become very important to you as time marches forward.

Law practice settings (the physical locations where lawyers perform their work) differ significantly and generally break down into the following two categories: law firm practices and "everything else." Although the opportunities in "everything else" can be very interesting and satisfying and should not be relegated to second place status, the truth is that the highest percentage of law school graduates start out at law firms. So that is where we'll start too.

Law Firm Practice

You probably think you know a lot about law firm practice because you watch TV. *The Practice*, *The Good Wife*, *Suits*—they all can be very entertaining.

But don't believe everything you see there. The real thing is a lot harder and does not include the same level of excitement most of the time.

A law firm is a group of lawyers who practice together under a common firm name. For example, 50 lawyers who practice together as XYZ are a law firm. The partners share profits and losses and operate as one entity. It seems like a fairly simple concept, but it can be very complicated operationally.

If a high salary is your objective, aiming for a law firm could be a good choice. Although there are other lucrative law practice settings, most of those jobs go to lawyers who have spent time at law firms first to get the experience they need to transition to those other settings.

For example, if you have never practiced in a law firm, getting an in-house counsel job or a high-ranking government lawyer position will be challenging. Businesses that hire in-house counsel and many government employers often seek out lawyers who have had impressive experience on "the other side" and can anticipate strategies from opponents. That kind of experience makes them very valuable in litigation, prosecution, and transactional settings.

A high salary can be very tempting. With the cost of law school today, many young lawyers have considerable student loan debt to pay off. They can do that a lot quicker with law firm salaries.

However, money is not always the key consideration for satisfaction in a law practice. Although money can solve a lot of problems related to the material world, it also can complicate personal issues like work-life balance and wellness. If you are interested in law firm practice, you need to look at it from all perspectives.

Law firm practice can be very stressful. Going to court can be anxiety-creating, and that is where many legal disputes in a law firm end up. Transactional work can be very stressful also, especially when there is a lot of money in a deal and so much at stake. And other practices also can involve the stress of business travel and difficult clients.

A stressful practice and being away from family can complicate personal lives and impact work-life balance and family relationships. And the performance requirements at law firms can also add to stress. For example, even if you knock it out of the ballpark in your early years at a law firm and make it through the first gate of partnership, you are likely to find that the expectations are raised with each new level of promotion. What starts out as high billable hours becomes billable hours plus high business development expectations and requirements.

Law firms are also very competitive environments and involve office politics to determine who gets what work and how profits are shared. Those kinds of competition and compensation disputes can lead to very unpleasant working conditions.

For all of those reasons, the private practice of law can be a very demanding career choice. However, it also is true that law specialties differ, and what may be the case in corporate law may not be the case in environmental law. It would be a mistake to make too many generalities because one law firm can differ significantly from another.

Apart from the demands and stresses of law firm practice, it is very rewarding for many lawyers. Law firms include a broad array of practice opportunities and mentors and interesting and exciting work, especially if a lawyer rises through the ranks. Litigators love the adrenaline rush of the courtroom, and transactional lawyers would not trade the thrill of closing the deal for anything. Other law firm lawyers are drawn to the structure of a law firm and being surrounded by other practitioners who enjoy talking about the law *all day long*.

Law firms come in all shapes and sizes. There is prestigious Big Law—google "Am Law 100," and you will see what I mean. These firms are typically *very big* (at least 500 lawyers—and as large as thousands of lawyers) and include offices in multiple states and usually in some foreign countries as well.

Big is not necessarily better, however. Big can be very impersonal, and it is not unusual for lawyers in the same office not to know each other. Or Big Law may provide all the opportunities you are looking for.

If you are interested in Big Law, you need to go into it with your eyes wide open. You will find that many entry-level lawyers find Big Law isolating and disappointing. Their experiences staring at computers all day long, without much interaction with colleagues (and, in most cases, no contact with clients) can be very limiting. It has been documented by American Bar Association and legal consultant studies that isolation and being ignored can lead to anxiety and depression.

Law firm managers are becoming more and more aware of these problems, but it is not clear that they are making much headway in solving them. Most work in large law firms is billed to clients by the hour, and the number of hours billed determines profits. So, the more hours billed by each lawyer, the better the profit picture. That leads to a very demanding work schedule.

There is a lot of opportunity in Big Law, but there also can be a lot of frustration and disappointment for young lawyers. It is a lot to think about. And it should not be overlooked that large plaintiff's firms, which traditionally bill based on contingent fees (when a percentage of recovered judgments, verdicts, and settlements goes to the law firm before distribution of the remainder to the client) rather than hourly work, can be highly lucrative practices that do not necessarily mimic the environments in defense-oriented settings.

Medium sized firms (typically more than 100 lawyers and with a regional focus) can be very satisfying places to work, and smaller firms hold an especially strong appeal for some young lawyers. A lot will depend on where you want to live and what firms operate in those geographic areas. Although a lot of work is billed by the hour in medium sized firms, there also are possibilities for alternative billing arrangements like contingent fees and billing rates that blend the two billing models.

Smaller firms sometimes are referred to as "boutique" firms and often are specialty practices (for example, an intellectual property firm that specializes in trademark, copyright, and patent work or a workers' compensation firm that specializes in ERISA work). Boutique firms can be very pleasurable places to work because of the friendly environment and the mutual interest in subject matters.

And then there are solo practices, where there is only one lawyer. Solo practitioners do not have partners, and, because of that, solo practitioners enjoy complete independence in terms of which clients they choose to represent and what hours they work. That can be very attractive to some lawyers. However, the downsides of solo practice include small matters that mushroom into matters too large for available resources, no colleagues in the office to consult with on legal and procedural issues, and the challenge of raising enough start-up capital for all of the requisite elements of setting up a small business. Those elements can include website designers, intellectual property experts, and marketing and public relations consultants, to name just a few.

For that reason, before you take the leap to solo, it is a good idea to check out some of the excellent websites explaining that practice.[4]

And today there is a growing trend toward "virtual law practice." Virtual practice refers to lawyers who are not part of a traditional law firm and are connected mostly by technology. They do not practice in a common office space, and their business models and profit sharing can be much more "creative" than in traditional law firms where partnership is the typical model.

Lawyers in virtual practices rely heavily on Internet research resources available to lawyers, and virtual practice particularly appeals to lawyers who enjoy isolated "at home" settings and seasoned lawyers who want to work less and keep more of what they bill. An informational interview with

---

[4] *See, e.g.*, https://www.nesl.edu/blog/detail/9-things-you-need-to-know-before-starting-a-solo-law-practice.

a virtual practitioner would be a good idea before jumping into this model of practice.

Alternative Practice Settings

And then there is "everything else." Here are some of those alternative practices and what they entail:

- In-House Corporate Lawyer: This practice is typically situated within a legal department of a large entity such as a public utility, bank, insurance company, real estate agency, manufacturing firm, hospital, or other large business. This practice can result in more flexible work schedules and no billable hours. Downsides include the necessity to adapt to a business culture that is different from a legal culture and the comparative unavailability of legal mentors. In today's legal environment, in-house salaries can be between 30 and 50 percent of what lawyers can make in large firm practices so other work-life considerations become very important in the analysis of suitability.
- Public Interest/Not-For-Profit Lawyer: This practice provides legal representation on matters involving discreet issues and underrepresented groups. Examples include issues involving families, children, education, preservation of natural resources, healthcare, equal justice, and more. It includes non-government organizations (NGOs) and charities. There are no billable hours, and downsides include a high concentration of regulatory oversight and constant monitoring of laws affecting the public interest or not-for-profit organization.

- Government Lawyer: Lawyers for government entities provide legal services within a very broad category of settings and agencies of federal, state, and local government, and include government prosecutors, members of regulatory commissions, and congressional staff lawyers. Part-time practice is typically more readily available in this setting than in some other practice settings, and the retirement and benefits packages are excellent. There are no billable hours, and downsides are lower salaries than law firm practitioners and vulnerability to political winds.
- Law Firm Consultant: This lawyer advises law firms on issues of productivity, client development, management, diversity, and hiring. Consultants can bill by the hour or by the project, and downsides include the need for prior law firm experience at upper levels of private practice and becoming branded as representing only certain segments of the profession.
- Academic: This lawyer has gained professor status at undergraduate schools or law schools. The work is attractive to lawyers who enjoy pursuit of knowledge within an academic setting, teaching, writing/publishing, and being in the presence of student populations. There are no billable hours, and downsides include the need for prior experience at high levels at law firms or other practice settings.
- Alternative Dispute Resolution (ADR) Neutral: These lawyers are sometimes referred to as arbitrators or mediators. Neutrals, like judges, do not represent a particular side of a dispute, and they hear and decide disputes outside the traditional

courtroom setting. Neutrals can bill by the hour or by the project, and downsides include the non-binding effect of some types of ADR and the need for experience at a senior level in a specialty practice.

My *New Balance* book includes more detailed information on law firm practice and alternative practice settings, including profiles of lawyers in those practices. The lawyers, who are profiled there, all started out in law firms and, for reasons related to work-life balance and passion for the work, transitioned to other practice settings.

Making tough choices about which legal setting fits you best is all about discovering what "floats your boat." So, especially with alternative practices, you need to identify where your true interests lie.

Sometimes this is expressed as "finding your passion." I understand, however, that finding passion in your work may seem like pie in the sky in this complicated and demanding world. I also understand that people in prior generations have placed too much pressure on finding a professional passion to pursue, as pointed out by Phyllis Haserot, an expert on multiple generations in the workplace. In content shared on her website Practice Development Counsel,[5] she states there that "You can't force passion," and counsels patience. She also quotes a millennial telling her that you get passionate about what you are good at and that it requires time and experience.

So, ignore the "passion" reference if you prefer. Just think of it as "job enjoyment and satisfaction."

No matter what you call it, the truth is that far too many lawyers simply do not even "enjoy" their practices and

---

[5] https://www.pdcounsel.com.

have little job satisfaction. They muddle through with little to look forward to but a paycheck.

You do not want to be one of them. You may know your passion early on, or it may take time to develop. It may derive from experiences in a law firm or it may involve finding other career paths to follow. But chances are that, if you find job enjoyment and satisfaction, success and enhanced feelings of self-worth will follow.

One of my contributors stresses that you give yourself time to find your passion. He says that it can take time to determine whether you really enjoy the substance of the work that you are doing. He quotes experienced lawyers as saying that you should not judge your career satisfaction in one year or even two. He further states:

> "Sometimes it takes a little longer to find the type of work that really motivates you. Be open to changing your focus early in your career. It's much easier to change your path earlier than later. The legal profession is challenging enough even if you love the work. If you don't enjoy the work, it can feel like torture. It's critically important that you enjoy the substance of the work you're doing. If not, make a change."

If you have a real interest in your practice, it will show. It will show to your colleagues, and it will show to your clients. It can turn hard work into something manageable and tolerable, and it will become a source of pride.

Think about your job satisfaction early and often. Think about it before you take your first job out of law school and think about it throughout your career.

If you cannot find job satisfaction in law firm practice, look at the alternatives. There are so many options to explore. It is a long career, and you want to spend it doing what satisfies you and makes you happy.

There are many articles and books written on finding a law practice that suits you. Among them, I particularly recommend *Beyond the Big Firm: Profiles of Lawyers Who Want Something More* by Alan Morrison and Diane T. Chin. There you will enjoy reading profiles of lawyers who left Big Law for something more satisfying.

Now that you know more about the variety of law practice settings, let's talk law practice specialties.

Practice Specialties

When you ask a lawyer what his or her practice specialty is, the question has nothing to do with the physical place where the lawyer works. Specialties are substantive areas of law like business law. Some other examples are:

- Tax law,
- Constitutional law,
- Criminal law,
- Personal injury law,
- Environmental law,
- Admiralty and maritime law,
- Health care law,
- Intellectual property law (copyright, trademark, and patent),
- Estate and trust law,
- Sports and entertainment law,
- Litigation (aka trial law),
- Appellate law,
- Franchise and distribution law, and
- Immigration and nationality law.

Law practice specialties are not limited to any one practice setting. For example, you can practice maritime law within a government setting and also in a law firm setting. You can practice criminal law as a government prosecutor, as a public defender, and also as a private practice defense counsel. You can practice health care law in a not-for-profit setting, a government setting, and also at a private practice law firm.

There are plenty of specialties for you to choose from when the time comes. Most young lawyers start out as generalists and take whatever work the practice sends their way. Over time, however, young lawyers discover specialties that are of particular interest to them, and they seek out that work in hope of building a practice around it.

Related Careers

In addition, there are alternative careers that are related to the law and draw heavily on legal skills and law educations but do not qualify as practicing law. Some of those include:

- Financial consultant
- Management consultant
- Lobbyist
- Pre-law or law teacher/professor
- Legal career coach
- Investigator
- Investment consultant
- Mediator
- Fund manager
- Realtor
- Labor relations specialist
- Contract manager
- Director of human resources

- Chief executive officer
- Risk manager
- Head hunter

The possibilities are expanded and tailored to your own backgrounds and expectations on the following websites. I think you will find that going through the exercises presented there to see where you fit best can be very helpful in your decision making.[6]

The subject of job satisfaction and careers related to the law was explored in a blog I read and enjoyed. I think you will too. The writer, a young lawyer, spent almost four years in a variety of jobs until she found what really mattered to her and fit her vision of herself as a professional. Fortunately for her, she had the internal fortitude to recognize her lack of passion for certain jobs and moved on until she found one that satisfied her. That was not an easy thing to do in what was then a "down" economy, but it worked out for her.

The following excerpts from the blog emphasize that what you do with your lawyer skills should be of far less importance at the beginning of your practice years if you use that experience to discover what fits you best.

> "Every time a job didn't work out, I felt like something was wrong with me. I internalized everything and it all felt like failure."

Does that sound familiar to you? Failing to find your passion in a work setting is *not* the same as failure. It just means you have not looked long enough and, perhaps, hard enough.

---

[6] *See* https://www.legalnomads.com/alternative-careers-for-lawyers/ *and* https://www.indeed.com/career-advice/finding-a-job/alternative-jobs-for-lawyers.

The writer ended up discovering her calling by founding a start-up company. Does that mean that she abandoned the law? Here is how she describes the transition:

> "I started out scared and the empowerment came later. I realized that I am not only capable of founding and growing my own startup, I think I'm meant to become a CEO. [I experienced] the realization that it's okay that I'm not going to have a traditional attorney job—that nothing is wrong with me for not wanting a traditional attorney job . . . I will always be an attorney. One of the reasons I am going to be a great startup founder and, eventually, CEO is precisely because I am an attorney."

This young lawyer conquered her fears and embraced her passion. Will you follow her lead? Or will you languish in a job you do not enjoy and eventually abandon your role as a lawyer out of ennui and job dissatisfaction? I hope you will choose to follow her lead. There are many ways to use your lawyer skills, but it may take some introspection and courage to find what suits you best.

Conclusion: A Call to Action

Success in the practice of law depends on good career choices, realistic expectations, a willingness to work hard, effective strategies for success, and the nature of the workplace.

If you have taken your career choice seriously *and* you have realistic expectations about the profession *and* you are willing to work hard *and* you pay attention to effective strategies for success, then you have lived up to your part of the bargain. Those are the things that I have tried to prepare you for in this book.

But that alone does not make for career satisfaction and success. The unknown for every young lawyer is the nature of the workplace. It is what too often disappoints and results in unnecessary departures from law practice and from the profession.

Unwelcoming and toxic practice settings disappoint, and uncaring managers and supervisors disappoint. Being ignored and left on your own to fail disappoints.

Millennials, who represent between 20 and 25 percent of practicing lawyers today, are often perplexed and disillusioned by the law profession. They can be made to feel abandoned and without recourse. Even those who have paid attention to survival techniques and skill mastery find themselves unhappy and insecure in what can be hostile practice environments. It is a very slippery slope from that point forward.

What often is overlooked by law practice leaders is that many of those disappointed and disillusioned young lawyers are still paying off large amounts of student loan debt, and, once inflated salaries help make a deep dent in that indebtedness, there is not much left tying them to the profession. It is then that they chance becoming part of the talent drain that threatens the law profession today. And too often law practice leaders disregard these bold road signs of danger ahead.

The way I see it, it really does not matter whether the law firm leaders of today think that millennial lawyers deserve more humanity in the workplace. And it really does not matter whether those same leaders think that revamping mentoring programs and adding strong skills development training is necessary for young lawyers. And it really does not matter whether those leaders think that Generation Z lawyers, who are just entering the profession, will deserve it either. All that really matters is that overlooking those issues will lend to a drain of young talent that could have been prevented.

Those who believe that focusing exclusively on huge and unprecedented profits is the only thing that matters in today's law practice are overlooking the damage that the threatened talent leaks will do to the profession. If middle-level talent dwindles and succession plans fail because of it, the leaders and managers of today will have no choice but to reflect and regret their resistance to change.

If those same leaders and managers are ignoring the projection that, by 2030, 75 percent of the workforce could be millennials, they do so at their peril. If those same leaders and managers do not recognize that millennials in the c-suites of business will be looking for millennial lawyers as outside counsel, they are not in touch with reality. Those millennials went to school together, hung out together, and they all speak the same language. They share familiarity and trust. And if those millennials in the c-suites do not find their ilk in one law firm, they will look to another.

Effective change and new programs to address deficiencies will take lawyers at the highest levels of practice to step forward and say *enough is enough*. It will take their wisdom and their courage to recognize that some of the current practices in the law profession are out of control and are creating disappointment, disillusionment, anger, and dismay among young practitioners that is not healthy for them, their families, or the future of the profession.

I share with you the recent sentiments of a boutique law firm leader, as reported by *Above the Law* on February 10, 2022, addressing the reasons his firm is making structural changes by developing an incentive program that reduces the focus on billable hours, increases focus on career satisfaction, and establishes a profit-sharing model where lawyers will be eligible to receive compensation based on the firm's month-to-month successes. Here are his words:

> "Our incentive program originated from the dissatisfaction with the class system, and the focus on billable hour requirements in Big Law. We want people to have skin in the game, which makes them more invested in the firm and their overall success and career.
>
> A lot of people are realizing that money doesn't buy happiness. It's about sharing purpose, learning and growing professionally, and participating in work that challenges you. And life outside of work is important too, because a happy life means being on your game at work."

This is a brave move. Although I understand the difference between boutique firms and Big Law, I also think the rationale expressed above has broader application than just small firms.

And if these kinds of initiatives are taken seriously, I believe there will be far less complaining from young lawyers. I think that they are rejecting an uncaring profession more than they are rejecting hard work. There is a very big difference.

I hope that these kinds of initiatives will become widespread. I hope that the profession lives up to your expectations, and I hope that you live up to your commitments.

And, most of all, I hope that you experience satisfaction and success in your careers—inside or outside the law. Good luck.

Postscript: The Best Friends at the Bar Website

When you think of Best Friends at the Bar, your mind probably wanders to college watering holes where you hung out with friends to talk about life. I know mine does, and that is one of the reasons I chose the name for my project. It is where I talk about the life lessons that are important to the success of young lawyers. And the reference to "the bar" just works!

In addition to the information included in my books and other publications, the Best Friends at the Bar website, www.bestfriendsatthebar.com, is an excellent source of information about and for young lawyers. There you will find an index to hundreds of blogs I have written over the past 15 years and indices to my programs, appearances and written work. You can buy my books there, and you also can sign up for my periodic newsletter to keep up with recent developments at Best Friends at the Bar and in the profession.

The information is all easily accessible using the tabs at the top of the homepage. I hope it will be useful to you.